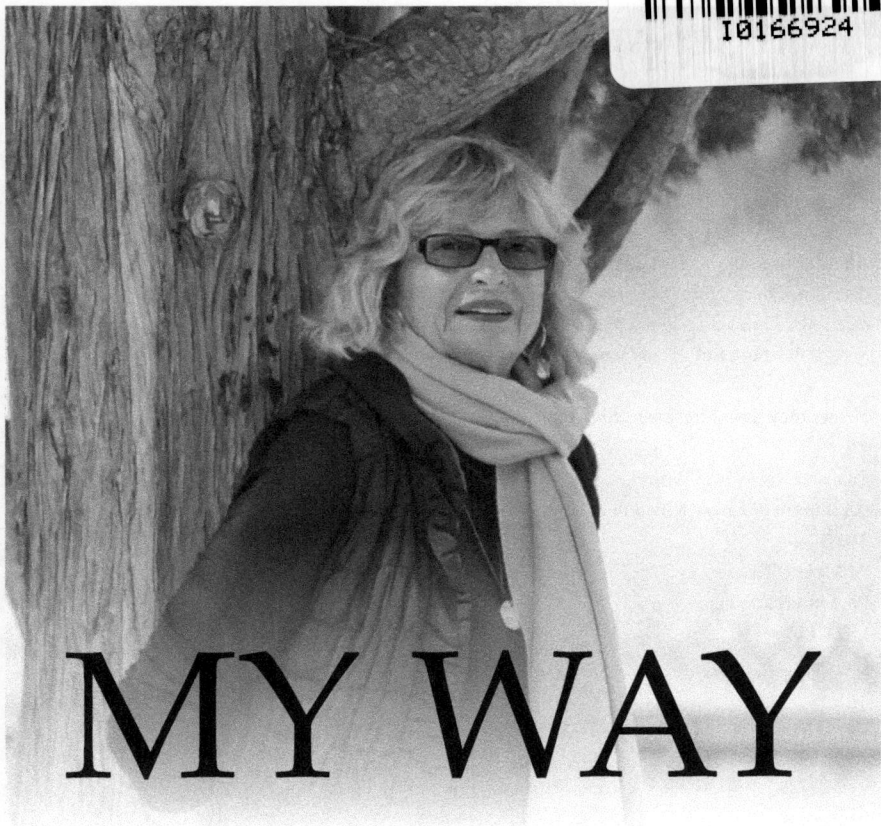

MY WAY

A quest across the world to find the secret code of happiness.
The inspiring journey of a woman's head and heart.

BETTY STEINHAUER
with Charu Bahri

MY WAY

Copyright © Betty Steinhauer 2020

ISBN 978-1-913170-21-9

First published in 2012

Published by Woven Word
An Imprint of Fisher King Publishing
The Studio
Arthington Lane
Pool in Wharfedale
LS21 1JZ
England

Cover photography courtesy of Vicki Mcleod
www.vicmcleod.com

"I have observed Betty's journey as a successful businesswoman, creator of her own inter-national charitable foundation, world traveler and frequent visitor to her beloved India. Betty shares this arduous journey from despair to triumph in her new book. Betty's vivid descriptions of her many trips to India help us to understand the large role India has played in her ethereal journey for inner peace. Betty's life is a rich model of perseverance in overcoming life's obstacles to find spiritual peace through hope and love."
- *Michael Levine, retired professor of economics and political science, Fresno, USA*

"I have known Betty for a relatively short time but it seems like I know her well. That's how she is. Exuberant, easy to get on with and ready to attempt anything - almost anything, I feel I should say. Quite a woman, this Canadian blonde, you might conclude, that goes around the globe meeting and befriending people. I also do know that there is a very serious side to Betty that focuses on what's important, on achieving tough goals she sets herself and has the strong determination that she will not deviate from once she decides on a course of action. Her spiritual inclination gives her a very soft side that packages all of her very nicely. You will oscillate between magnetic excitement and alarm when you meet her!"
- *Nizar Juma, Group Chairman, Jubilee Holdings Limited;*
past Chairman, Board of Directors, Aga Khan Health Services (Kenya), Kenya, Africa

"Working with Betty Steinhauer on the boards of both the McMichael Canadian Art Collection and St. Elizabeth's Health Care, I came to know a passionate advocate of social good. My Way relates the tale of her remarkable journey to her goals of social responsibility, personal fulfillment, and spiritual growth."
- *Noreen Taylor, Chair, Charles Taylor Foundation;*
Chair, St. Elizabeth's Health Care, Toronto, Canada

"As long as I have known Betty, she has been an inspiration to me for her ideas, her willingness to help and her ability to transform ideas into action; but more importantly, for her ability to traverse so comfortably, both universes – the intellectual and the emotional, East and West, intention and action. She is adept at bridging the culture of the East where the seeds of seva or service have been sown, and the culture of the West where those seeds have been nourished by the right combination of drive, determination and mobilising the right people to create meaningful change. Through this book, we come to understand the experiences and influences that led to Betty's unique voice and in that process, better understand what it takes to find our own."
- *Upkar Arora, Managing Director, Illumina Partners Inc, Toronto, Canada*

DEDICATION

To Percy Axtell, my late Dad, with much love. Though you left me far too soon, I still feel your presence, sitting on my shoulder and looking after me. My best memory of you is you playing soccer with my friends in the schoolyard, your bushy blonde hair blowing in the wind.

To Jody and Julie, my children, with love. You are both independent women who I am enormously proud of. I admit that I was a different sort of mother, which is not to say that I love you any less. I just didn't have a role model.

To Spencer, Dawson, Megan and Benjamin, my grandchildren. I love you to bits. You are very fortunate to have four involved parents in your lives. It is a joy to watch you grow.

ACKNOWLEDGMENTS

Hillary Clinton said that it takes a village to raise a child. Well, this book of mine has taken the world to get done. My friends, who have read all or a part of the manuscript, and advised me, include Barbara in Australia, Tamasin in New York, the late Meredith in Vancouver, Michael in California, Denise the world citizen, Honna in Boston, Elin in Iceland, Micki in British Columbia, my late friend Hal who worked with me on the manuscript as we traveled the world, and Beth, who put so much effort into this project knowing how dear it is to me. You all listened to me, and heard me go over and over the reasons why I was doing this. I hope I haven't missed anyone. I'm sorry if I have.

To Professor David Staines, who read the first draft and said I had a story, but rewrite, rewrite, and rewrite. To Noreen Taylor, a special thank you, my fairy Godfriend, who spent countless hours reading rewrites, writing comments, and helping me stay focused. Charu Bahri, the story-teller, as she likes to be called, thank you for your focus and persistence. To Dadi Janki and the Brahma Kumaris, who have accepted me as a friend and who have taught me so much about myself!

To Rick Armstrong, Samantha Richardson, Rachel Topping and all at Fisher King Publishing, thank you for your support.

To all my friends around the world who have given me so much and who are my family in many ways. Thank you to everyone from the bottom of my heart.

And finally, how can I forget, India, you are forever a part of me! Thank you.

PREFACE

I write this on a warm, sunny March day, sitting on a park bench in the Brahma Kumaris Global Retreat Centre in Oxford, England. It is a beautiful manor home surrounded by acres of gardens on the banks of the Thames, just the right setting to help me reflect on how this all began. This book started 15 years ago as a letter to my Father, telling him that I was okay and that I had a good life. Then, it evolved, because people used to say to me that I had the perfect life – a beautiful home, flashy car, chic clothes, opportunities to travel and the good health and will to make the most of these, and so on. I wanted to explain that I hadn't had a perfect life. But I found it hard to do so. I wanted to say that life is perfect in spite of its imperfections. But that was impossible to say without going into the details of my own life. Perhaps, I wasn't ready for that exercise at the time. This book is an attempt to share of myself.

My life has been remarkable in many ways, and the journey is still continuing. I have been through many tough situations, physically life-threatening instances as well as emotional ups and downs. My philosophy of life is to learn every day, forgive people and myself, and move on. Speaking of forgiving, it is easier to do when you are not judgmental of people. People all over the world, rich or poor, want the same things - a roof over their head, enough food to eat, a healthy family, safety for their loved ones - and we all face the same insecurities and make the same mistakes. When I made mistakes, or individuals in my life made mistakes, and a door closed as a result, I looked for and found another door, and walked through. Sure, someone was watching over me, maybe God, maybe my Dad, maybe both. Even so, life is what you make of it. And when you look back, you will realize that even when you thought that your life was not perfect, 'perfect' as most people would define it, it still held the potential to help you grow. I love the game of life and I love the opportunity to beat the odds and make good.

In the past two years, I have begun to feel truly independent and free, and that means a lot for someone who has put in a lot of effort to impress people. Now, I'm myself and I'm comfortable in my own skin. The process of writing this book has helped me reach this position because in getting it all out, I have gone over bits and pieces of my life that I didn't understand at the time. I have made sense of it all, in retrospect. You know what they say, hindsight is always 20/20. Maybe I needed to put myself through this exercise because I've made a habit of pressing ahead in the face of adversity without spending time to dwell on the whys and wherefores. Still, writing this book hasn't been easy. It may not come across so, but I am a very private person and with this book, I have let it all hang out. Why? I don't know. What will people think? I haven't a clue. I have changed some individuals' names to protect their privacy. Larry, my ex-husband, agreed to let me use his real name if I used mine (which I thought was funny). There was never any doubt about using my own name. This book is MY TRUTH. There's no escaping that.

INTRODUCTION

When it comes to the secret of travel, perhaps no one in recent history put it better than Marcel Proust, a French novelist who, around the turn of the nineteenth century, said, 'The real voyage of discovery consists not in seeking new landscapes but in having new eyes.'

I agree. What greater learning could there be than looking at life with new meaning? And if you must travel, what voyages could be more meaningful than those that help us gain new perspectives?

It seems to me that if you possess the right spirit, you can learn a lot from being exposed to different cultures and people. At least, that's how it's been for me. My travels have taught me to accept people as they are and not be egoistic to assume that I understand situations that are different from circumstances I have found myself in. Some of my visits to distant lands have also brought back memories of my own life. Sights and sounds from places far from home have as though opened a closet crammed with memoirs describing my earlier years, forcing me to relive moments I'd relegated to the back of my mind, and sometimes, to reflect about the way I've lived my life. These reflections of my own life coming from unfamiliar places and people I thought I had nothing in common with, besides being members of the human race, have reinforced my belief in the fact that we, the people of this world, are one family.

Considering that all the noteworthy chapters of my life have come to life again during my travels, not to haunt me, but to help me come closer to understanding the meaning of oneness, I have chosen to start this, my take on my life, with a memorable visit to India in 1990, the year I was badly bitten by the travel bug. Memorable, not only because it was the first of twenty-three visits to the country, but also because I came back with the most precious gift of all - the gift of love (got you there, bet you thought I'd say enlightenment).

Yes. People carry back many things from their travels - souvenirs, memories of cherished moments, and so much paraphernalia, but for me, that visit to India stands out for having introduced me to my soul-mate. What more could any die-hard romantic possibly want?

There's something else. Two and a half thousand years ago, there lived a Greek playwright called Euripides, who said that experience and travel are an education in themselves. For me, someone who missed out on formal higher education, and the sort of person who learns best in 'live' settings, or direct from the horses' mouth, as I like to say, my travels are as though my degree (and considering that I've traveled to all the seven continents, I think of myself as no less than a doctorate). To be well-traveled is not synonymous with being well-read, but it gets pretty close. It's about being global in outlook, which is something I admire, as opposed to having an insular perspective, since it's the attitude you need to be able to call the world your home and look upon its people as your family.

ONE

The last thing I wanted was to get the runs before setting foot in India. Friends had warned me to watch what I ate, and I took their advice very, very seriously. Blame that on my nerves – I was traveling to India for the first time and didn't know what to expect. Sure, I'd flipped through the Lonely Planet India guide the week before, reading up about the cities and towns I'd be visiting. But was that enough?

Three years earlier, during one of my earliest trips abroad, I'd learned the hard way that it's not always a good idea to succumb to exhaustion when you're on a flight, or to be too trusting of strangers (even if their credentials read well), or to travel unprepared. I remember I was en route to Israel with my friend Joyce when the first of these nuggets of wisdom dawned on me. I was in holiday mode, and at the time, that meant that I was good for a shuteye anywhere.

There I was, sleeping peacefully when a soft murmur woke me, I opened my eyes to see, much to my consternation, a rabbi leaning over me. Ouch! I was about to shriek when I realized that he was saying his prayers. It turned out that he needed to face the sun to commune with God, and apparently, I had the best seat on the plane for the purpose... and he didn't feel the need to wake me up...

Unable to go back to sleep after this rude awakening, I sought to pass the time by chatting with my fellow passengers. That's when I discovered that the consul general from Toronto (my home city) was on the same flight. He seemed a friendly sort of guy, and possibly found me likewise, for he requested me to carry a bag for him through security. I was far from being a seasoned traveler back then, and my happy-to-help self agreed to help him out without so much as batting an eyelid... only to almost die of embarrassment when the bag leaked wine all the way through the airport. Seeing people's eyebrows rise at the trail I was leaving (it reeked of alcohol), I wanted to shout out, 'I'm not an alcoholic, it's the consul general.' But I kept my mouth shut.

That was only the start of it. The next day, I had two pairs of jeans stolen from my hotel room and when Joyce and I went out in the morning, someone locked the wheels of our car, leaving me fuming and fretting and determined to vent my frustration. That meant walking two miles to the nearest police station to lodge a complaint. When I got there, however, I didn't quite find what I was looking for - an orderly station manned by kindly officers who would understand the plight of this tourist who was visiting their country for just a few days. Nopes. I found three young recruits brandishing guns or sitting back, guffawing over what must have been some lewd joke, legs coolly tossed on their desks. I can tell you I was taken aback - they looked like a bunch of teenagers playing 'Police'.

From the looks of it, the 'teenagers' were as taken aback as I was, and as I found out later, they had good reason to be so. I walked in, an unescorted female in her early forties, blonde (which in itself put a question mark on my brainpower), wearing a black leather jacket and black jeans... I stood out like a sore thumb from the locals on the street, and in those days, tourists visiting Israel would only travel in groups accompanied by a rabbi, who'd also book them into the right hotels (where they wouldn't have their clothes stolen) and organize their local travel (so that they wouldn't have to bother about parking in the wrong places) and so on (but of course, I only found out all this when it was too late). Sure, I was also a successful Canadian businesswoman, divorcee, and mother of two grown-up girls, but those punks (pardon me, I refuse to call them anything else) didn't know that, and I doubt it would have made any difference to how they proceeded. I was a treat for them and they ended up having a field day at my expense, insisting that I be strip-searched for a US$15 ticket. I was simmering by the time I walked out of the station but couldn't figure out who to complain to.

As it happened, luck favored me, and I actually got to have the last word on the subject. I had a dinner date the same evening, and my date sat me adjacent to the police chief of Jerusalem - you can imagine the earful he got. I'd learned a valuable lesson too - never travel to a foreign land without doing some homework. That's why I had my nose buried in the Lonely Planet India guide the week before, to read up whatever I could about India.

TWO

I was grateful for one consolation that left me decidedly calmer than I'd usually be before embarking on a visit to a foreign land. Anthony or Ant, my next-door neighbor back in Toronto, was traveling with me, and he'd been to India many times before. So all in all, I felt pretty much in control, which is how I like to be. Except that my stomach was growling.

I'd kept up a personal tradition of eating a plateful of smoked salmon at Terminal Three in Heathrow, which meant that I was not hungry when lunch was served an hour after take-off. Now we were five hours into our flight from London to Bombay (it was renamed Mumbai in 1995 but this part of my story dates back to 1990, and I'll stick to Bombay throughout), and I'd just finished reading a fascinating story about trekking in the Himalayas in enRoute, Air Canada's in-flight magazine. I could no longer ignore the fact that I was starving.

Friends who'd been to India had advised me to avoid street food (that means roadside food stalls even though it sounds like food picked off the street) but had said nothing about in-flight meals. So I used my own judgment and that said, 'Take it easy.'

One of two gracious-looking cabin crew sashayed down the aisle, the swishing of the pleats of her sari announcing her arrival, as she walked in perfect balance and poise as air hostesses do. I peeked at the plate of delectable-looking Indian snacks she was carrying to a rather noisy group of kids sitting two rows behind me. In spite of the packaging, the aroma of the food hung in the air as she walked past - it reeked of oil. It was the poor woman's umpteenth walk down the aisle, as she and her colleague scurried back and forth catering to the whims and fancies of passengers who to my ears seemed to be demanding travelers out to make the most of the free snacks (low-cost carriers and budget travel fares had yet to become a rage back then).

Another growl from my stomach reminded me of my purpose. I stopped the air hostess on her way back, somewhat apologetically because I genuinely felt she had a lot on her hands and asked her if she something *light* to eat. 'Sure, would a salad be alright?' she asked, and then asked me if I'd like to sample the Indian cuisine. 'It's not spicy,' she added.

Hmm. Indian cuisine tweaked to suit a western palette. But no. It may not have been spicy but it would be loaded with calories. Sensibility overcame me. I wasn't accustomed to eating Indian food, had never dined at Ameya or Kamasutra, well known Indian restaurants in Toronto (speaking of which, with a name like Kamasutra, the ancient Indian Hindu text widely considered to be the ultimate guide to sex, any restaurant would be well-known), and reluctantly thought that I'd leave sampling Indian cuisine for another day. I politely declined. Then I had a think about the salad as well. Salad is something I usually avoid when traveling - because you never know how well it's been washed and all of that. But I thought Air Canada should be safe.

Two minutes later, the air hostess returned with a plate of salad. Ten minutes after she set the plate down, I rested my head back satisfied, loving the taste of the Indian mints (they're served as breath-fresheners) that I was now chewing, as content as the passengers who had by now stopped clamoring for more snacks.

Taste buds are what we make of them and that is why seasoned travelers (like me) learn to appreciate new aromas and flavors as they venture forth to savor the world. Having said that, I must confess that I am not particularly fond of exotic cuisines from far-off lands, no thanks to my weak tummy. Experience (they say experience comes from bad judgment and in my case that has meant spending many hours in smelly toilets in unfamiliar places) teaches frequent fliers to play it safe as far as food and water are concerned. The last thing you want is to reach a new destination, miles away from the comforts of your home, with an upset tummy. And however much you travel the world and enjoy new cuisines, there is no replacing your earliest to-die-for's, perhaps those chocolate chip cookies baked by a loving grandmother or whoever, essentially tastes that represent the last vestiges of a long-lost childhood.

As for me, my taste-buds were largely shaped by my girlfriend Barb's mother - she used to bake seven apple pies in one go. Don't ask me why seven, maybe that's all that would fit in her giant oven. I'd sit at the kitchen table and watch her, relishing the thought of digging into some apple pie. My earliest gastronomical experiences at home, however, were somewhat more down-to-earth. That thought made me both happy and sad, as I thought of Dad, and Mom, and Yorkshire pudding.

Most of my memories of my mother dating back to my early years revolve around her being sick. She had a bad case of rheumatoid arthritis and her disease would flare up every so often, leaving her struggling to get through chores and look after me. That's why Dad encouraged me to look after myself from an early age and set a good example for me by looking after his own needs and ours. Dad would rush home from his job as a machine foreman with a tire manufacturing company and waste no time in making himself useful at home. He'd cook up simple meals, the likes of beans on toast (very British), roast beef Yorkshire pudding (I loved that), hot dogs and macaroni and cheese. Essentially, quick-fix meals that an overly busy dad could rustle up with some assistance from his helpful (ahem) daughter. I guess that's why I haven't tired of eating Yorkshire pudding even after all these years. The dish always brings back fond memories of bonding with my father in our cozy kitchen while Mom would just sit and stare into space.

I thank Dad for his positive attitude. I don't recall ever seeing Mom and Dad fighting or yelling. And his never complaining about the extra work is honestly the only reason why I never grew resentful about the fact that Mom couldn't do more for me, and never complained about why she wasn't more like my friends' moms. In fact, now, when I look at the broader picture, I realize that accepting Mom as she was, was the start of a life-long habit of accepting situations coming my way without complaining. I learned that it helps to focus your energies on getting out of uncomfortably difficult situations. Brooding over what could have been is such a waste of energy.

THREE

The empty plate lying in front of me brought me back to the present. I wouldn't have minded dozing off (I lost that ability post my Israel experience) and envied Ant for his ability to switch off at will. He was fast asleep on the reclined adjacent seat, eyes closed, hands neatly folded on his lap, even snoring gently. He looked quite the part of the sleeping beauty, undisturbed by the baby crying ahead of us and the hum of conversation coming from all directions. 'If that is what meditation can do for you, it would be worth traveling to India to just learn how to meditate,' I said to myself. Though that was not exactly why I was airborne, five hours away from Bombay.

This is how it came about that I was on my way to India:

A few weeks earlier, I had met the Dalai Lama, but before you make too much of that, let me clarify that I was neither practicing nor studying Buddhism, nor do I have an interest in Tibetan political history. We met simply because I was involved in planning a few events at the University of Toronto that he was taking part in.

I guess many other people would have treasured the opportunity to meet the Dalai Lama in person. But in all my trademark honesty, I'd have to say that our meeting was not an earth-shaking experience. His Highness came across to me as a regular guy with a sense of humor and the ability to talk about any aspect of spirituality. I bet not many people would describe him that way, but there you are. That's how it was for me.

The morning after this anything-but-out-of-the-ordinary experience, I met Dadi Janki (dadi means 'elder sister' in Sindhi) at Ant's place. Dadi Janki, I was informed, was one of the founding members of a worldwide socio-spiritual organization having its headquarters in Mount Abu, a small hill town in the western Indian state of Rajasthan.

The previous evening, Ant had briefed me about the meeting, saying it was an informal gathering and so there was no dress code as such. 'Just dress comfortably,' he'd said. He also told me that Dadi held no management degrees but was one of the finest leaders that he had ever seen. I'd shrugged my shoulders in response. I meant to say, 'That's okay for you to say, but isn't seeing believing?' I was respectful of the lady and appreciated the fact that she'd come a long, long way from Sindh, a province in present-day Pakistan, which is where the Brahma Kumaris took seed in 1936. But I wanted to figure out my feelings for her myself. I was still thinking about meeting the Dalai Lama a few hours before - nothing had come out of it. I had seen no visions; I had come away with no inspiration to study Buddhism, nothing. Not that I'd gone into that meeting expecting something, but then, you never know. I always thought that encounters with spiritual leaders stir you to action, even if it's only momentary, and you run out of steam after that.

There was pin-drop silence in Ant's living room when I entered - in a black tracksuit only to face a sea of pristine white. They were all wearing white clothes. Not white and some other color. Just white. I stood out like a sore thumb.

Dadi was meditating with a small group of people. The curtains were drawn and the lights were off, though an eerie reddish lamp lit up the room. Ant motioned me to an empty chair. The next ten minutes were agonizing. They meditated, while my mind flitted from here to there. I'm sure that my train of thought didn't qualify as meditation, even though I spent a few moments engrossed in speculating what people think about when they meditate. Then the lights came on and I swear I let out a sigh of relief.

Now I expected a talk, perhaps with the help of a translator. But no. It was time for more meditation, personalized meditation if you please, meaning that Dadi called us each to sit in front of her, one by one, and as far as I could make out, twisting and turning in my seat to look upfront, she held each person's hand and looked them in the eye for a few minutes, and said... nothing. Ouch! How would I survive that? Surprisingly, when my turn came, I don't recall feeling the minutes pass. I just remember my heart beating really fast and shaking from head to toe, which was a new experience for me, something that I don't recollect ever doing even while being ticked off by my most frightful school teachers. *She's special,* said an inner voice. This diminutive elderly woman dressed in a simple starched white sari was special. I can't pinpoint exactly why I felt that way, so let's just say that I could feel it in my bones, or was it my heart or my gut? Well, it was the kind of feeling when you feel strongly about something and inexplicably know that you are right. I must confess that my experience with Dadi Janki was part of why I was traveling to India.

FOUR

I'd often toyed with the idea of visiting India. Ant had suggested it on a couple of occasions as well, and every time, until now, I'd held back, not because the idea didn't appeal but because I wasn't sure if the time was right.

India was more than just a place to visit for a holiday; it was the ultimate destination for spiritual enthusiasts, which I most certainly was not. I was too much in love with life to be seeking nirvana. Nor was I in search of a Guru. That is not to say that I had no interest in spirituality, for I did. But my approach wasn't as serious (might I say) as Ant's, and it was a far cry from the likes of Dadi Janki.

A few years earlier, I'd visited Esalen at Big Sur in California. Esalen is an amazing spiritual center, the ideal place to be in if you need time out to journey within. I visited the center to take courses in vision painting and in wisdom, inspired by a need to understand and connect with my spiritual side - perhaps as a result of feeling fulfilled in the material realm? Esalen seemed to be the right place for a beginner like me to start a spiritual journey. And it lived up to its name. During my stay, I found myself painting an inner vision - a globe surrounded by a chain of children holding hands. It would take many more years for that vision to pan out in reality. But I enjoyed the course nevertheless, in all my ignorance of what life had in store for me next. My stay at Esalen meant a lot to me for another reason - I made a new friend... Michael.

Michael taught political science at the University of Berkeley in California and was taking part in a retreat at Esalen. When I first saw him reading a book in the dining room, I remember making a mental note: 'cute guy'. Then by a miraculous twist of fate, we were introduced and talked for hours on end. I found him really laid back as compared to most of the men I knew, very free-spirited and well-read, which set the ground for long-drawn conversations that led us nowhere but drew us closer to each other. No, I've got that wrong. We eventually did end up somewhere - in a hot tub. Call that a spiritual retreat, Betty style.

Michael and I were lovers for a very brief interim before we went our separate ways, promising to stay in touch... and we did live up to that promise. It wasn't like you meet someone, have a fling and that's the end of the story. I found a friend for life in Michael, someone I can share everything with, from relationship issues to the most mundane things. We've kept in touch ever since - that's over two decades, which says a lot - chatting for hours on the phone every week. And not so long ago, I attended his second marriage in California.

For all my escapades with Michael, I considered my time at Esalen well spent. It had given me a taste of quietude and reflection, baby steps to spirituality, but essential all the same. Was that enough to take a bolder step, as Ant suggested?

The meeting in Ant's home had aroused my curiosity about what makes creative, spiritually aware young people tick. Ant was at the time president of Young Rubican Advertising. He, his sister Denise Lawrence and another UK-based follower of the Brahma Kumaris, Michael George, had all practiced Rajyoga meditation for many years, and I remember being struck by the clarity of their minds. These vibrant individuals spoke with confidence about the self, the meaning of life, and other stuff that most people only start questioning when they get much older if they do at all. I wanted to know more about these young, seemingly evolved personalities. For me, that was another good reason to travel to India.

There was more to it, too. By the age of forty-seven, I had reached a point in my life where I realized that the West didn't hold all the answers. Somehow, Western lifestyles didn't express the level of happiness and hope that I had seen during travels to less developed places in Asia and Africa. I had also lost faith in organized religion. And I was willing to accept wisdom from any quarters, and genuinely believed that I was more likely to find it in the East.

FIVE

Organized religion. It doesn't appeal to me. My problem with organized religion is that it is bound by too many rules and is not accepting - is even fearful - of wisdom that falls outside the scope of its established rules. I first got wind of these restrictions when I was in my teens.

I used to enjoy voicing my opinion during discussions with the minister of our Baptist Christian church. At least, I did, as long as I was allowed to express my thoughts freely. On one occasion, I got into a discussion about evolution with the minister and brought Darwin's theory into the exchange. That was it. The minister pursed up his lips, looked me up and down as though I were an alien, and in no uncertain terms, expressed his disapproval for my 'boldness' (that's what he called it). 'Fine,' I said to myself, 'If you can't explain the Bible, I refuse to accept it.' Since I was not willing to accept the concept of Adam and Eve and the Garden of Eden without understanding every aspect of it, I slowly distanced myself from the Church.

I wasn't hurt about what had happened - you get used to change fairly rapidly at a young age. Nor did my parents mind me dropping out of the church choir. I don't recall Dad ever speaking to me about religion as it is, but he would nonetheless religiously drive my mother and me to church every Sunday, and wait outside. So we were all happy to trade our church-going Sundays for ice-cream Sundays.

I may have thought that I'd never have anything to do with the likes of priests and formal places of worship ever again, but as life turned out, this episode didn't mark the end of my engagement with organized religion. Wise people say that you should never say never, and I agree... because a few years down the line, I was ready to convert to Judaism, all for the sake of love...

I met Larry at the wedding rehearsal of a girlfriend, where I was the maid of honor, and he, the best man. My ensemble - a pink suit, Jackie Kennedy style with black fur trimming on the collar and white kid gloves - ensured that I received more than my share of appreciative glances that day, and yes, from Larry too.

His attention was by no means unwanted. Larry came across as a really nice guy - he had a great sense of humor and a lovely smile and had everything going for him at work too. He had just started out on what I sensed would turn out to be a promising career - a chartered accountant with IBM. His folks seemed nice people too - they were comfortably off, lived in a nice house on the right side of the tracks, and were members of good clubs. I'm sorry, do I sound like a gold-digger? Like every other girl in my time, *all* I wanted was the white picket fence, a perfect life with a loving husband and children in a large house in the suburbs. Back then, I didn't believe that it was too much to ask for.

But like every love story in the movies, there was a snag - Larry was Jewish. Not that he or his parents minded him marrying a non-believing

Baptist Christian, but his grandparents were still around and very much involved with family affairs, such as approving their grandson's choice of wife. They were devout Jews...

'Put a Star of David around her neck, and we'll pass her off as Jewish,' said Larry's dad after giving the matter some thought. It didn't work. His grandmother was very bright and figured out what was going on, but she was a very lovely woman and never let on except to me. Still, I realized it was highly likely that the rabbis would have found out too, if not before, then at the time of our marriage, so I tried to make things easier by suggesting that I convert to Judaism. Anyway, I genuinely believed that a family that prays together stays together.

Converting to Judaism was easier said than done. Back then, it just wasn't the done thing (I'm not sure if it's the done thing now, but I know for a fact that the process is less cumbersome). I was one of the first few people to convert to Judaism in Toronto, and if that doesn't sound like a big deal, I converted to the reformist Jewish sect as that was all that was 'allowed' at the time.

But first, I needed to learn about Judaism, Jewish history, and modern Jewish events and culture. Larry's family arranged for me to meet with rabbis twice a week over the next three months, which was interesting as the rabbis were talkative and bright. In the run-up to my marriage, I went all out to show my interest and actively participated in services dealing with contemporary issues.

My disenchantment with Judaism started round about then, even before I'd 'officially' converted. I saw members of the congregation talk throughout the service - which was so rude - and on the Jewish high holidays, families were more concerned about what service you had a ticket for and what new outfit you planned to buy to show off at the synagogue.

My friend Barb got married around that time (she was a Roman Catholic), and of course, she asked me to be her bridesmaid. I was so happy for her, and remember we were merrily planning our color-coordinated outfits when we got a call from the priest - he'd heard about me being a bridesmaid and disapproved. 'You can't be a bridesmaid at a R-o-m-a-n C-a-t-h-o-l-i-c (he stressed the words) wedding because you're converting to Judaism,' he said. What a stupid rule. Once again, religion was showing me its true colors, and they weren't pretty. If I kept the faith alive in spite of all the hypocrisy (which I did), it was *only* because I had my marriage to think of.

SIX

Fat load of good it did me, though. My belief in organized religion crumbled slowly, alongside my marriage. Larry and I failed to love, comfort, honor and protect each other till death do us apart... I know those aren't the vows we took as a Jewish couple but isn't that what every marriage is about?

I never looked upon our drifting away from each other to mean that we failed as individuals. We failed at being together, and most of all, to comfort each other when the going got tough.

It's funny, but as I look back, I realize that my wedding dress could have been a harbinger of things to come.

I bought it at a budget store that I was introduced to by Estelle, my future sister-in-law. I was actually going someplace on a streetcar when I ran into her, and she was on her way to the largest budget store in town. Estelle needed help to make ends meet back then - she'd married Larry's brother while he was still in medical school. As he refused to take any financial support from his family, the two were always short of money until he graduated and started working.

I tagged along simply because I'd never been to the store, but I was a good one for buying my clothes on sale. At the store, I was lucky to find a beautiful white wedding dress... I tried it on... it was a perfect fit, and at only $9.98, it was also a steal. Sometime later, I saw the same dress being sold in a bridal store for $125 - I think that's when the wonder of the bargain I had struck hit home! The only drawback in my discount store piece was that it was a little dirty around the bottom - sure, the dry-cleaner took care of that before my wedding, but the fact remained. My wedding dress had been pristine white but marred by a little dirt when I picked it up, beautiful but with shades of ugliness - that's why I say it could have been an indication of life to come. Of course, I didn't know what life had in store for me back then. Thank God for that.

Married life was a piece of cake in the beginning. Larry slogged in true IBM mode. I had a job too. Over the next three years, we saved up to make a down payment on the home of my dreams – where else but in the suburbs. Call that the icing on the cake, which was topped by a cherry soon after that when I got to know that I was expecting. The pregnancy was unplanned, but I was very excited about having a baby all the same. I read every book on parenting and looking after babies that I could lay my hands on. And nine months later, we welcomed a bundle of joy, our daughter Jody, into our lives. She was one of the most placid babies that ever blessed this earth - she slept well and ate well and was no trouble at all.

I felt very much in control of life. Was that a good thing? In retrospect, I realize that the feeling of having it all – a happy home, great husband, perfect daughter - it leaves you on a dangerous high, extremely vulnerable to take your circumstances for granted, making the ensuing lows that much harder to cope with, when they come. And just as certainly as pride comes before a fall, every good thing comes to an end.

For us, the turning point was the birth of our second daughter, Terri Anne, on July 25, 1968.

Terri was a much easier birth than Jody, but as a second-time mother, I found her unnervingly easy to care for. I would toss and turn in bed at night, expecting to hear a wail ring out any moment demanding my attention, but no. She would just sleep and sleep and sleep, and hardly breastfeed - this wasn't how it had been with Jody. I spent a lot of time that first month after she was born on the phone with her doctor. 'Something's wrong,' I said it what seemed like a million times, but I just couldn't seem to convince him. It was only during her first monthly check-up that after a lot of badgering, he told me he heard a heart murmur.

So? Not being a medical professional, that meant nothing to me. We were advised to take Terri to the Sick Children's Hospital - they wrote 'referred for further diagnosis' on her case sheet. They may as well have prepared me by saying - 'to see her tortured' - that's how horrifying it was. Doctors prodded her and poked her and drew what seemed like more blood than she had in her, and all the while, we could do nothing but stand and stare, our hearts in our mouth. What else could we have done? Then finally, the prognosis - Terri had two holes in her heart, because of which her blood was circulating the wrong way, and all her blood vessels were blocked.

'She will not live out the year. I'm sorry.'

I always wondered if the doctor found it as easy to say those words as it sounded.

Now the natural order of life for every species on this planet is that children outlive their parents. When the reverse happens, it's devastating. The blow is all the more hard to bear when it is delivered slowly. That's the low that hit me, again and again, over the next six months.

At first, ready to grasp at any straw, we sent Terri's medical records to a heart surgeon who was performing one of the first few heart transplants in Texas. 'She'll die on the operating table,' was his considered response. Another letdown. That's when the truth began to sink in - Terri would not live out the year.

We 'decided' to let Terri live for as long as she could without pain. Decided? The truth is that we had no choice.

Terri stayed on in the Sick Children's Hospital where the staff indulged her every day, more, I believe, to indulge her broken parents. They dressed her up in pretty dresses with bows in her hair and carried her around like a mascot.

Larry and I spent all the time we were allowed in the hospital, only to ease our biting conscience by rushing back home to Jody. We were caught up between the girls. Terri needed us and Jody back home, under the watchful eye of my girlfriends and neighbors Florence, Jo-Anne, and Judy, was only two. Her world had been turned upside down too. How could I possibly explain to her that we weren't abandoning her?

SEVEN

How do you prepare to see your child die?

Do you cry incessantly? Do you reach out for support? Do you curse your fate?

In spite of sharing a common aim - getting through the darkness and back into the light - two individuals coping to survive the same tragedy might respond in entirely different ways. That's what happened to Larry and me. Larry genuinely had to believe that Terri would get better somehow while I had to accept the truth - my baby was dying, and there was nothing I or anyone else could do about it. It was the start of a deepening rift between us. I understand that we both had to do what we had to, to survive, but we no longer seemed to be talking the same language.

I longed for a shoulder to cry on - even though I didn't have the time to sit back and grieve. I was desperate to share my anguish with some family member, but my husband refused to accept reality and his parents - well, their way of coping was even harder for me to comprehend - they chose to avoid the issue altogether. They refused to visit Terri, saying that they didn't like hospitals, nor did they ever offer to babysit Jody. Terri may as well have already been dead. Our relationship grew increasingly strained from that point onwards. The circumstances left me feeling alone and isolated.

I believe that Jody was the only reason I pulled through - knowing that I had a baby back home who needed me helped me keep my sanity, and face the next day, and the next... All the while, I was desperate to find a way to keep it all together and kept up the pretense because I believed that I couldn't seem tired to myself or my immediate family - Larry, Jody, and Terri. No. That would never do. I had to be strong to keep us going, to ensure that Terri got the best care possible and didn't feel the pain. It didn't matter to me if I came across as vulnerable to others around us. That time was about us.

As I write this many years later, I realize that a part of me was in shock. I responded to the chaotic situation as best I knew how - by putting up barriers around me to try to make myself immune to the sense of inaction that comes from grief-induced numbness. I also realize that I've used this survival method time and again... a challenge just has to rear its head, and there I am, withdrawing into myself to cope, to do whatever it takes to make sure the people I love make it through the dark night.

Terri steadily lost weight – born at seven pounds, two ounces, she died at four pounds but had gained in length. Think of photographs of malnourished African babies that you see in magazines - that's what Terri looked like, all skin and bones. On December 27, we finally made what is most certainly the hardest decision I've ever made in my life. Terri's doctor wanted to keep her alive on machine support as she couldn't breathe without tubes, but I put my foot down. The idea of my daughter leading a vegetable-like existence... I couldn't do that to her. If nature had had her way, Terri would have been dead already. We faced the fact that the time had come, and together, Larry and I pulled the plug.

It is a time of my life that is vivid fifty years later, right down to Terri's blue dress and the pink bows in her hair. We should have buried her, in keeping with Jewish tradition, but I didn't have the strength to put my baby in the ground. I'd been through that some years earlier when Dad died. I'd cried and cried for days on end, and finally said, 'Never again'. So Terri was cremated and we had a small service in the rabbi's study.

The months of hoping against hope were over. There was no more running around to do, and that is when I became aware of just how tired I was - emotionally drained, physically exhausted, and mentally fatigued. No longer able to hold it in, I let it all out. I cried. I cursed my fate. I cursed Terri's fate. I plagued every rabbi I knew with questions they had no answers to.

Why must people suffer and feel pain?
Why couldn't Terri have died at birth
Why did this have to happen to us?
Why?
Why?
Why?

One senior rabbi had visited me at the hospital. I found some comfort in his words now too. But it wasn't enough. I needed answers that made solid sense. Once I had the answers, I figured I could move on. But they weren't forthcoming. The silence was more comforting.

But not the silence that came from my husband. Larry just couldn't accept that our baby had died. He wanted Terri's room to stay the same, whereas I wanted to throw out her clothes and everything that had been hers. Nor was I comforted by the studied silence of some of our friends, people who had never shared a word of sympathy with us when we were going through our darkest night. They had stayed away from us all those months that Terri lay sick in the hospital and now too, they completely ignored the fact that our second daughter had died, for God's sake. We started entertaining again, trying to bring some semblance of normalcy back into our lives, but though these friends came over when invited for dinner, they didn't even bother to offer their condolences. They studiously avoided the subject - as though Terri had never existed. I resented that, how could they...

Other people around me would philosophize about God taking away Terri to be an angel. I hated such talk too. Some would say you come out stronger and wiser from sad events. I didn't quite agree with that either. Losing a child is with you forever. It's a pain that's hard to comprehend, and in my opinion, that's what makes it worse - sometimes, you have to move on without really understanding 'Why?' More often than not, you only think you understand more. That's when something snapped inside - I'd had it with organized religion. Religion gave me no answers, no reason to get on with my life. And I had to move on because, somewhere deep inside me, I believe that we're meant to look forward, not backward and that we were meant to live happily and somehow get over the grief that lies in our paths as best as we can.

EIGHT

"Good afternoon, this is your captain speaking, with just a little flight information. We're flying at an altitude of 37,000 feet, and our airspeed is 400 miles an hour. We'll be coming in to land in Bombay in just over 12 minutes. The temperature in Bombay is 33 degrees centigrade, and the humidity is 60 percent. The seat-belt light will come on exactly ten minutes from now. On behalf of your cockpit and cabin crews, we hope you enjoyed your trip and will fly with us again soon."

My India sojourn was about to begin.

Bombay was a revelation, but not the kind that makes a favorable impression. The unraveling of any expectations I had harbored about my visit started as soon as we stepped into Sahar International Airport (now Chattrapati Shivaji International Airport). First, we negotiated serpentine customs lines and floors stained with dirt and grime (weren't they *ever* cleaned?), and then it was the heat. Oh, the heat. The unbearable October heat hit us as we walked out of the terminus towards the taxi stand.

There were no air-conditioned blue Cool Cabs back then, so it was a regular black and yellow taxi I slid into. Even with all the windows rolled down, it felt like a furnace. Five minutes later, we'd barely crawled out of the gates of the airport, but I was feeling desperate for a shower.

"How long will it take?" I shouted out to Ant over the deafening traffic.

"A while."

He smiled. I groaned.

Sweat ran down my forehead, neck, and legs. I tried to take my mind off my growing desperation by looking out of the window. There wasn't much to see though I learned a lot about how traffic works (or doesn't) in Bombay

- not a subject I am particularly interested in - in the 20-mile journey to our hotel.

Back home in Toronto, if you're lucky to reach an intersection when the lights are green and drive on at an average speed, you can more or less be certain that you'll sail through the next few crossroads. There's automation and precision for you.

Here, however, the traffic lights turned green and red and green and red, again and again, even before we reached the intersection to actually cross - that's how long the traffic lines were. We'd just inch our way forward nearer the crossroads hoping (after I figured out what was going on) to cross the next time, or maybe the time after that... So *this* was India's commercial capital. Huh. In my mind, I was finding it hard to figure out how the people got anywhere, let alone got any work done at all.

The 90 minutes it took to reach our destination was nothing short of traveling to eternity, many times over. The waiting was made worse by the beggars. Not that it was the first time I'd seen beggars or been approached by many. But during one such halt, an elderly beggar put his arm inside the window... I screamed, startling Ant, the driver, and the poor leper. I didn't mean him any disrespect, but it was the first time I'd come that close to a leper...

Unlike the taxi, my mind was in overdrive. I tried to slow it down and lift my spirits by playing a mind game. I began envisioning the place we were going to stay in. I'd heard and read a lot about Indian hospitality, and let my imagination run wild, as wild as the utter chaos outside the taxi window, seeing plush carpets, crystal chandeliers, cut glass windows, carved heavy teak furniture, wrought iron grilling, uniformed and turbaned bearers, exquisite (not too spicy) food...

Bad idea. Expectation is spiritual suicide. I've learned that the hard way, many times over in my life - it's not the kind of lesson that you learn in one go. Our minds are so accustomed to expecting from people or places that it takes a while to realize how futile an exercise expectation is. In *A Course in Miracles*, spiritual teacher Marianne Williamson says that 'infinite patience brings immediate results.' Patience is power personified, the energy that manifests our dreams. Whereas I was being and doing the opposite - I may have been imagining the best, but I was driven by my impatience, my disgust at being in a hot and humid inferno. And that is why I was let down by my expectations.

I expected the works to be laid out. I expected to experience Indian hospitality at its best. Instead, I stayed in a dark and dingy hotel that had crows flying around an inner central courtyard. The dark interiors were a far cry from the bright sunshine I had been hoping for. I screwed up my eyes as we entered, trying to adjust my eyes to the depressing interiors. Peering here and there, I saw dust and grime in every corner. Ugh.

NINE

As I dozed off that night, I made a mental note to research five-star hotels in India before my next visit... though, at that point, I doubted the likelihood of ever visiting the country a second time. What for?

The next day brought forth more firsts for me - I saw monkeys adorned with jeweled collars. No, not in a circus, in a temple. Then we visited the Haji Ali mausoleum, the shrine of Sayed Peer Haji Ali Shah Bukhari, a rich Muslim merchant originally hailing from present-day Uzbekistan who made Bombay his home in the fifteenth century.

The legend goes that the Saint died on his way to Mecca. Since he had directed his followers to cast his coffin into the Arabian Sea, that's what they did. Miraculously, the casket carrying his body floated back to the shores of Bombay, where it got stuck in the string of rocky islets located about 500 meters from the shoreline, in the middle of Worli Bay.

The islet is linked to the city by a narrow causeway, about two-thirds of a mile long. Access to the shrine depends on the tides - as the causeway is not bound by railings, it gets submerged during high tide. In fact, the walk to the shrine with the sea lapping on both sides, and the shrine itself, a brilliant specimen of the Indo-Islamic style of architecture, are considered highlights of a visit to Bombay.

It sounds romantic, I know. Trust me, it was anything but that. 'God' is big business in India - a land where faith healing means much more to the common man than it does in any Western nation. I don't recall what day of the week it was - thousands of people of every faith and religion visit the shrine on Fridays, the equivalent of the Sabbath day in Islam - but I remember the walkway as being lined with hundreds of squatters, people with missing limbs or diseased beyond belief, who had traveled to the shrine to seek the Lord's mercy. Picking my way through while taking care not to hurt anyone, I felt that I had never seen so much hardship and misery stemming from poverty and disease in my life. Even my exposure to the inner city side of Toronto came nowhere near this. I felt my eyes well up and desperately wanted to sit down somewhere quiet and sob for all the people suffering in the world. But I didn't want to sit among *these* sufferers and so sniffled and slowly walked along.

Naturally, there were beggars too, out to make the most of feelings mollified by a visit to a house of God. They danced around, trying to catch my eye.

"Don't give anything to anyone. You'll be swarmed by them," said Ant. I walked on, looking down at my shoes and slid gratefully into the waiting taxi, hardly noticing the driver wiping perspiration off his forehead as he started the engine.

I couldn't stem the flow of my tears for all of our drive back and only managed a weak smile when Ant pointed out a lone policeman standing in the center of a traffic intersection to me. He was wildly waving his hands around. It honestly looked as though he was pleading for help in making sense of it all. Of course, that was a figment of my imagination. He was just doing his job - even if not very effectively.

TEN

The next day we flew to the city of Ahmedabad, from where it was a five-hour journey by road to Mount Abu. Now a five-hour drive back in Canada would be a breeze, especially for someone who loves driving as I do. Not so in India. We traveled on the most pothole-riddled road that I have ever seen in my life, something that had to be felt rather than seen, to be believed. Every limb in my body was shaken by the time we reached Mount Abu, but that's something you'd only understand if you've actually traveled by road in India before the last decade when the government rolled out national highway projects that have significantly improved the quality of the country's vast road network.

Mount Abu, the only hill station in the western Indian state of Rajasthan, is nestled in the Aravali range of mountains. It's not an easy place to reach - the closest airstrip is Ahmedabad (Udaipur is a second option now), and the nearest railhead (for those who are courageous enough to brave traveling by Indian Railways) is the town of Abu Road, at the foothills of Mount Abu. All said and done, it's pretty much the back of beyond, and as the bird flies, not too far from the border with Pakistan.

The drive to the foothills was awful, but the last thirty minutes or so sort of made up for the poor run on the highway. It was a beautiful drive up the mountain - the hills were green, and we saw monkeys (again), but these were really cute. They were sitting on the walls by the side of the road, hoping that passing cars would stop and leave them some food (and to my delight, I saw a few tourists feeding them sandwiches).

The township of Abu is located at an altitude of about 1000 meters, which isn't very high considering that it's a hill station but since it's placed at the edge of the Thar Desert, it experiences extreme climatic conditions - temperatures fall to freezing point in winter and touch forty degrees centigrade in summer. As far as I know, and I've visited the place about a dozen times (no kidding), October, November, February, and March are the best months to visit. But I'm running ahead of my story...

That first time, and indeed every time I've visited the reclusive mountain-top town since I was in Mount Abu as a guest of the Brahma Kumaris, a socio-spiritual organization having Rajyoga meditation study centers in countries across the world. My first impression of the place I stayed in, a building called Sukh Dham (meaning, the abode of happiness), in stark contrast to my impression of the hotel in Bombay, was that it was very clean and well-maintained, right down to the freshly whitewashed walls of the buildings.

My room was small but functional. It had everything I needed - a bed (the mattress was very hard, so I asked for an extra and slept on two), a bedside table, a bathroom fitted with a Western toilet (thank God), provision for a shower (a luxury), two buckets and a mug to help the showering process (how?), and a balcony looking out to rock formations on the mountains beyond (the height of luxury). Sure, it wasn't the executive suite of the Taj Palace Hotel. Nevertheless, it was far more than I expected (I wisely didn't spend the drive to Mount Abu playing mind games envisioning the place).

After washing off many layers of dust and grime accumulated during our journey, I was taken on a guided tour to familiarize myself with the place. Everything I saw - the dining halls, kitchens, bookshop, telephone exchange, visitor center, meditation rooms, and so on - looked pleasing. The place was run by volunteer devotees, mostly youngish men dressed in kurta - pajamas (popular attire with Indian men) who presented a picture of starched primness. And these young men, believe it or not, worked under the guidance of a group of ladies who headed the institute and were in their seventies. I was pretty impressed. I wondered how the ladies managed to pull it off - the place was so well-run. And the kitchens especially caught my fancy. They were spotless and served excellent food that was mercifully not too spicy. There was also a special chai (tea) kitchen and a candy kitchen if you please. It was very much like being in a fairy tale.

ELEVEN

The first morning, I attended a workshop by Michael George, who I'd met in Ant's place, in the company of about a hundred other participants from across the world. This should be good, I thought, sitting back to enjoy his talk.

The lady sitting next to me smiled. I politely smiled back.

Then she leaned in and whispered that she was the sheriff of Dade County in Florida.

"Great," I whispered back, signaling that Michael was about to start his talk... (and so would she please shut up).

But no, she had something else to say to me.

"I'm going to kill myself."

I stared at her. Let me honestly confess that I'd thought a bit about the sort of conversations I'd have on my first morning in this spiritual complex... and this wasn't even the last. It was all I needed to set me off.

I couldn't possibly sit out the lecture - this lady needed help. My help. That meant a lot to me because I am a great one to help people. Call me a global helpline or whatever, but it's true - when I get the whiff of a needy situation, it stays with me until I do something to change the situation for the better. It doesn't matter to me if the person needing a prop up isn't a friend or a family member. I'm happy and ever-ready to go over the top for people I don't know. The sad part is that sometimes my efforts backfire on me, like when I do too much, or the recipient doesn't appreciate the help of a stranger. Here, however, someone was actually calling out to me.

Rising to meet the challenge head-on, I slunk out and sought out Ant. Since I was in an alien environment, I needed some guidance myself. Was there a psychiatrist on hand who could counsel the lady? Ant would know.

I don't think he was too happy to be called out of the lecture hall. Still, he heard me out and then said, "It's all part of the drama. It'll be fine. Don't worry. You're not here to help the lady. You're here to help yourself. Go back and enjoy Mike's lecture."

What?

I stared at him in disbelief. Had he lost his mind? How could he not be bothered? Had he heard me correctly? This wasn't the caring Ant I knew, or should that be, the Ant I thought I knew?

I tried to reason with him, but Ant wasn't having any of that. He walked back into the hall, indicating that I should too.

But I couldn't. No sir, I had a job to do and wouldn't rest until I'd done it... so I sought out two people I'd met earlier that morning at breakfast - twin brothers from Australia, Michael and Joe. They'd listen to me, really listen, I mean. Not brush aside what I had to say.

Or so I thought.

They said that it would be fine too, leading me to wonder if they had somehow got wind of what Ant had said, and they would not be upset about whatever happened. Then almost as an afterthought, they said that the woman would not shoot herself.

Huh.

There was nothing left for me to do but walk back to the lecture room, where Mike had finished his first talk and was now answering people's questions. I sat in the last row, taking in none of the discussion, wondering why Ant, Michael and Joe hadn't freaked out when they'd heard what I had to tell them. Craning my neck, I also saw the lady in question sitting calmly, listening to the lecture. I just didn't get it.

TWELVE

When something bothers me, I question why. I investigate and fidget until I've figured out whatever I need to know. Then, I can rest in peace. Not before. And I don't like postponing what I can do today for tomorrow. That's me. I forget that morning does not dawn in a jiffy. It takes its own time. And some things take time to understand.

At that point, I wanted to know if Ant, Michael and Joe had a different handle on life. To an onlooker (me), they seemed to be more in control of life than I was, and yet, they didn't need to seem to be in control... And the purity of the place - this may sound odd, but it left me in a rough space. Oh, it attracted me for sure, but it was a shock to my system. The pure vibe of the place and the people I met was so removed from anything I'd ever seen or experienced.

I thought and thought and thought, and yet, please understand me when I say that I couldn't keep a single thought in my head. If it was the chaos outside the taxi windows in Mumbai, now the confusion inside my mind was threatening to push me to the verge of a breakdown. These people were unlike any I had ever met in my life. As the minutes, then hours ticked by, my mind grew weary of thinking, so tired that it couldn't lull itself to sleep. Nor did I have the strength to take part in any more discussions.

Two whole days passed by, and I just sat or lay on my bed, doing nothing, thoughts passing through my mind but not staying. My hosts were very kind. They didn't press me to do anything. They even sent a British psychiatrist, also a follower, to see me in my room. Not that she could do anything for me - she just saw that I wasn't having a fit of madness or anything like that, and then left me to get my act together. My newfound friends served me endless cups of steaming chai and cookies in my room until I felt calm enough to venture out again.

It was dinner time when I stepped out of my room again. I made my way alone to the huge dining hall and helped myself to some French fries and steamed veggies. The Brahma Kumaris encourage what I'd call mindful eating or eating in the remembrance of God, so I tried to concentrate on the food on my plate instead of chatting with the Australian architect sitting to my right. The place on my left was empty.

About halfway through my meal, I felt a warm embrace and heard someone say, "You're fine, my child." It wasn't the architect's voice, so I looked around expecting to see - maybe Barbara, another Australian I'd befriended. But there was no one standing anywhere nearby. Strange. The experience had lasted not more than a few seconds, but it threw me into a flap. Again.

I needed help, so I sought out Barbara and narrated the episode. She said, "You've had a vision. Huh. I've been meditating for so many years, and I've never had a vision, and here you are, visiting for the first time, and you have a vision." So... that was what it was. I thought Barbara must know, after all, as she said she'd been practicing Rajyoga meditating for years. That didn't stop me from freaking out; however, only this time, I didn't seek refuge in my room. I went to the meditation room, where I told God in no uncertain terms that I was angry with what was happening to me and to stop it. Not quite the words I would use to converse with Him in Canada, but there, at the top of the mountain, I felt close enough to Him to speak my mind freely. After I'd finished giving vent to my feelings, I sauntered back to my room, feeling so calm, which was unusual. I had one of the most peaceful and refreshing nights of sleep in my life.

Over the next few days, I made more friends, Tamasin and Robin, Barbara's daughter and ex-husband, and Frank and Margaret. They were all from Australia. I also met many more wise, creative Indians and foreigners, all followers, many of whom I count as the brightest people I have ever met in my life. I felt very fortunate to interact with them and really appreciated the conversations we'd strike up. They were much more meaningful than the mindless chatter that goes on in cocktail parties.

Finally, I felt relaxed and might I say it, at home. I really came into my elements during the remaining days of my trip, questioning a lot of the stuff I learned from the Brahma Kumaris. They preach celibacy, and that really mixed me up. I couldn't relate to the 'soul consciousness' they practiced, which suggests that you experience no desire for physical gratification if you experience yourself as a soul. Romance and love (and yes, making love) were important aspects of my life, and I was not prepared to give any of that up. But I couldn't deny that some of the other things they preach made sense. The Brahma Kumaris believe that time is cyclic, not linear. That appeals to me. They say that spiritual energy in the soul gets depleted as the time cycle spins and consequently, the quality of human life falls. According to them, humanity is rapidly reaching the end of the time cycle, and this will coincide with upheaval in many forms - strife, the breakdown of economies, government failures, environmental disasters, and whatnot. The balance will only tip, so to speak, when a sufficient number of individuals dedicate themselves to self-evolution and enlightenment. That will coincide with the start of a new time cycle.

Three decades have passed since my first visit to Mount Abu. During these years, the economic, social, environmental, and political condition of the world has worsened in front of my own eyes, leading me to wonder if there is more than a sliver of truth in their philosophy.

THIRTEEN

When I booked my ticket to India, I reckoned that I couldn't possibly travel so far and not see its most magnificent architectural marvel and symbol of love, one of the seven wonders of the world, the Taj Mahal. The Taj didn't figure on Ant's agenda - I sort of expected that but it didn't bother me. I was happy to make my way to New Delhi and Agra alone. Though I must confess that I'd come close to canceling the reservation after my Bombay experience. So thank you, Providence, for giving me the good sense to hold out... My stay at Mount Abu miraculously revived me, I felt on top of the world, confident that I could take on whatever India had next in store for me.

The management of the hotel (decidedly better than the one in Mumbai) I stayed in, in New Delhi, arranged the trip. Since I had very little time on my hands - my return flight to Toronto was later that night - it was only a flying visit to Agra and back. Call it the typically touristy outing: when you take in more sights, sounds, and flavors than you can process, then you try to make sense of it all a fortnight (or whenever) later when your holiday is over, only to find that you remember very few details, though the fragrance of the place stays with you for much longer.

I left the hotel in Delhi at four in the morning and reached Agra three hours later. I don't recall much of the city, probably because I couldn't see much through the tinted taxi windows, which I insisted on keeping rolled up with the air-conditioning on full blast. But I can say the opposite for my first glimpse of the Taj. I vividly remember walking through the main entrance and being struck by the imposing size and splendor of the mausoleum. The feeling only grew in intensity as we walked down the pathway leading to the tomb, and became one of sheer amazement as we entered. I could go on and on about the exquisite inlay work, but frankly, no words could even begin to describe the vibrant colors of the precious stones set into designs carved in huge slabs of pristine marble. The Taj has to be seen to be believed. There's another reason why I will pass over that description and get to the point...

Which is, the beauty of the tomb aside, I was struck more deeply by the feelings the emperor must have had for his wife. Sure, my guide did his best to impress me, babbling on in broken English about 'King Shah Jahan's most beloved wife, Mumtaz'. Little did he know that his words set me thinking, so much so that I asked for time out, and sat lost in a train of thought on a bench in the lawns in front of the Taj. Not that famous bench Lady Diana was photographed sitting on, alone, the marble mausoleum standing majestically in the background... But like the vulnerable princess who split up with Prince Charles a few months after she'd visited the tomb of love, I still hadn't found my soulmate.

My soulmate, I figured, would be a special someone, someone with who I'd share a connection from before (maybe a previous life), whose eyes would meet mine, and we'd instantly know that we were meant to be together. We'd be perfect together. We'd share a love that would last till eternity. We wouldn't fight and we'd always understand and accommodate each other's needs without having to resort to those clichéd one-liners of married couples - 'We need to talk', 'There's something I've been meaning to say'...

Get the point?

The way I see it, most men and women can only imagine perfect love. That's something coming from me because it's not as though I've ever felt the lack of love in my life. I mean, from men. Up until that day, I considered myself very fortunate in my relationships for having married for love and gone out with interesting men. But the imposing monument that it is, the Taj Mahal brought home a bitter truth. I still hadn't found my Shah Jahan. Sigh.

When I was writing this book, an acquaintance suggested that it should be about the men in my life. 'Why?' I'd asked, somewhat suspiciously. That would sort of make sense if I were, say, Marilyn Monroe. Why me? Sure, the male member of the species has been important to me - I'm a sucker for romance, sweet nothings whispered in my ear, caresses to die for, the first touch of lovers, feeling in perfect unison with the man in my life... I can't deny that fact and considering the many men I've had in my life, my acquaintance thought that my life had revolved around my relationships. But no.

My life has been far more than a steamy potboiler. Agreed, I've had my fair share of men, but each relationship, it seems to me, has represented only one facet of my life while it's lasted. My man of the moment, so to speak, entered my life for a purpose. Or to put it as a friend once said to me, some people enter your life for a reason, for a season... and if that sounds too self-serving, let me clarify that it's not as though I entered any of those relationships thinking about getting something out of it, and then moving on (to the next). I mean, I was thinking about getting love and companionship out of each relationship but then, doesn't everyone think so? I was referring to the moving on part. Irrespective of whether the relationship dated back to my life before my marriage, or was my marriage itself, or happened after my divorce, I entered it with an open mind, genuinely wanting to get close to the man and take our twosome to the next level, and the next. I wanted to make it work. And like every die-hard romantic, I believed that my partner would be there for me forever. If my relationship fizzled out, it was either because a) once I got to know the man, we realized that we were not made for each other and therefore not suited to be together forever, or b) we were great together at first but as time went by, we grew, as people do, but sadly in different directions, which made it impossible to stay together as lovers any more, or c), the man died (I know this sounds sad, but it's true).

FOURTEEN

Frank. Brian. Norman. Larry. Harvey. Tyler. Shah Jahan... No, no Shah Jahan had ever been a part of my life. As I sat on the bench, mulling over love, the names of some of my past lovers flitted through my mind. None had even come close to feeling like my soulmate - not even Larry, my husband of twenty-two long years. A strange feeling came over me as I wondered if I was right to believe so. Memories flashed by, and I found myself searching deep inside to figure out if I had misunderstood the potential in any of my relationships.

Frank was the first guy I went out with when we were both sweet sixteen. Frank was oh-so-cute, Italian (which explained his good looks) and like me, very good at bowling. We had something else in common too, something that was decidedly more intense than vanity, which helped us bond - Frank and I were both at home in the rundown parts of Toronto. My family had lived in a little house in Long Branch, Toronto, across the railway tracks. Frank was from a similar background.

It meant nothing to us that the evening strolls we took to get to know each other meandered past industrial lots crowned by smokestacks billowing fumes into the sky. We understood where we came from and it didn't matter because we meant to make it good. That's why I believed that we were made for each other. But at the age of sixteen, I wasn't thinking about my soulmate, boyfriend is more like it. And to my sorrow, Frank and I didn't have the opportunity to grow to think that way because our relationship was cut short by tragedy...

Frank died just a few months after we got together, in a car crash - his car slammed into a brick wall. In case you're wondering, yes, he was a fast driver, and yes, I used to worry about him, but I could never have imagined that it would come to this.

The moment when I heard about his accident has stayed with me all these years - a bunch of us were up at the bowling alley when one of our friends came running in and said there had been an accident and Frank was hurt... By the time I got there, the police had cordoned off the accident site so you couldn't see a thing. All the police were saying was that the young man was dead. 'Surely not,' said my sinking heart, and as a last shot, I beseeched a higher power to work a miracle, 'Please, please, please let it not be him.' But it was. My Frank was dead. I was in shock. Dad had died the year before, and now another person I cared for was dead.

I felt as though my worst nightmare had come true, and that's a horrid feeling. I sobbed and sobbed and couldn't stem the flow of tears. Barb came home to tell me when and where his funeral was being held. She also said, 'He burst the jugular vein in his neck,' and somewhat falteringly added, 'They're saying that the makeup doesn't cover... it, but his family is insisting on keeping the casket open in the funeral house.' I looked up at her, but she lowered her eyes so as not to meet mine and asked, 'Are you sure you want to go?'

I couldn't possibly not attend Frank's funeral, and just as certainly, I couldn't see him in that condition (I never found out why his family insisted on keeping the casket open). It took me all of a night of alternately sniffling and dozing to figure out that the only way I'd stay collected during the service would be to ensure that I couldn't see his body. I decided that I wouldn't wear my glasses when I visited the funeral home, and I'd sit in a corner and not go up to see the body unless his parents called me up. Mercifully, they didn't. I just sat in a corner, sobbing my heart out.

That goes to show how inexperienced I was in matters of the heart. I hadn't reckoned that feelings go much beyond the physical senses. So what if I couldn't see beyond two feet on the three visits I made to the funeral home? Just the thought of having lost him hurt so much, and I sobbed and sobbed throughout the service.

When disaster strikes, Nature sets in motion every recovery mechanism it possesses to right the wrong. Moving on is the natural order of life. Humanity has recovery coded into its genes, as I slowly found out. In time, I moved on too, though I'm not sure you ever completely recover from past losses. At least, I feel as though everyone I have lost still remains with me in spirit, in my heart. But at that tender age, my life stretched out in front of me, and I would be lying if I said that I didn't want to feel loved again.

FIFTEEN

So when I was ready to look reality in the eye and felt somewhat more composed about what had been, I succumbed to Brian's advances. Brian was the wiry sort of slight build and medium height with wavy brown hair and piercing eyes. He was a colleague from my early working days who was a couple of years older than me. I'll always remember Brian as the guy who introduced me to art and culture, concerts, the opera, and the finer aspects of life. We enjoyed each other's company, though when we weren't able to get 'serious' about each other after a few dates, we broke off with no hard feelings on either side.

Norman came next (pardon me if it sounds like I was dating one guy after another; I assure you it wasn't as bad as it reads). Norman was quite an imposing personality - six feet tall, crowned by a mop of brown hair, and from a very rich family. He wanted to marry me. But it would never have worked. Don't get me wrong, Norman was nice and fond of me, and I liked him too, even if he was a tad boring, rather prim and proper, and serious-looking (a combination of the fact that he didn't smile much and wore horn-rimmed glasses). That's why I went along with his feelings, thinking that I'd grow to feel as strongly for him, in time. After we'd been seeing each other for some time, I consented to visit his home for dinner. I knew that he wanted to introduce me to his family, presumably to take our relationship to the next level. And I needed to know more about him to figure out if I could grow to love him the way he cared for me. It was an unforgettable dinner, a date that showed me in no uncertain terms why I was not cut out to be Norman's wife... I remember we were chatting on the sofas in the living room when the butler rang the gong for dinner. I jumped right out of my chair when I heard the sound simply because I had no idea what was going on. It may sound frivolous, but that was it. I couldn't marry Norman. I'd make myself miserable trying to fit into his world, and it was more than likely that my misery would spill over to him.

Though at that moment, when enlightenment (so to speak) dawned, I felt miserable at the thought of having to explain my point of view to Norman during our next date. He was so intense, how would he take my backing off? Thankfully, Norman took it well, might I say better than I'd expected (maybe my jumping out of the chair had done it for him). I was so relieved about that because the last thing I ever wanted was to hurt him, or any of my ex-lovers for that matter, by parting ways.

SIXTEEN

That brings me to another must mention. The bitterness that many relationships end in really gets to me. It hurts me when men and women who once professed undying love for each other decide to go their separate ways, and then say that they can't bear the sight of each other, or can't stand each other's company anymore, or say nasty things about their ex behind their back, or... you know how it is.

I decided early on, that's not how it would be for me. I can dig the fact that a relationship is not working, and therefore even the most gorgeous twosomes fizzle out. But why create a song and dance about separation and get bitter just because you discover that he is not the man you thought him to be? No one compelled you to get together, and so, once it is obvious that you can't force the relationship, why blame the other for your bad judgment, or for having changed since when you first got together?

I know, I sound so wise. But let me clarify that I'm as human as the race is known to be. Though I managed to stay cheery when the relationships I had before my marriage ended, it was another story when Larry and I parted.

Then, I was shattered. During the twenty-two years we were married, I had grown into a clingy, needy wife who was unabashedly dependent on her husband. That's why it took all the reserves I had, and a lot of help from my friends, to stay afloat in the days after I walked out. Still, the beauty of even that miserable situation was that I couldn't blame Larry for feeling the way I did because dependency is one of the things I'd wanted from my marriage. I'd wanted a shoulder to lean on. I'd wanted a man to make life easy, and to be true to Larry, he fulfilled that part of my expectations during the years we were together.

It's just that I hadn't reckoned with the fact that I wouldn't always want the same things. When I married Larry at the age of twenty, I didn't have an opinion about many aspects of life and the world. I was happy to be a housewife. Two decades later, however, having experienced more of life and the world, I was a far more opinionated person. And I wanted more out of life than being a home-maker. I'd also experienced some success in my career and wanted to get ahead in that aspect as well.

But Larry disapproved of my career, which was weird because he'd initially been very supportive of my business - in fact, the idea had originally been his. Though when I started out, we both had no idea of the demands the business would make on my time. I ended up keeping very busy from the word go, and as time went by, Larry grew increasingly discontented as I acquired a reputation for my work. It grew to a point where our second income, mine, helped pay for family holidays and a chalet. Larry resented that. He still hankered for the happy-to-be-clingy-and-agree-with-husband-on-every-matter woman he had married. But I was no longer that person and believed that I was entitled to my growth. At that point, I'd have accepted Larry turning around and saying that he was entitled to carry on his life with someone who better fitted his worldview. Only that didn't happen. To my despair, Larry grew bitter, probably because he'd never thought that I'd muster the courage to walk out on him.

SEVENTEEN

In its later years, my marriage had reduced to a 'dead' twosome - we no longer spoke the same language, and we no longer felt happy for each other's achievements. In fact, we couldn't stand each other's company. It reached a point where I'd make a beeline for the bedroom as soon as dinner was over and stay put because I couldn't take any of what was going on. It's amazing how a soured relationship can reduce you to a shred of your former personality, but that's how it was for me. Our marriage was so obviously doing nothing for either of us... leading us to look elsewhere to satisfy our needs... And though, for a long time, I'd felt the need to stay on for the girls, I finally woke up to the fact that our verbal exchanges created an extremely unhealthy environment for them. But standing up to Larry and putting my foot down would take a lot of courage, more than I possessed (or so I thought). As it turned out, I first needed to get away from him to muster up the strength to walk out on him.

That's why I used to look forward to every opportunity to travel, thinking that I'd come back stronger, able to put an end to it all. I remember one of my last trips just prior to my divorce was to Dublin, Ireland, for a conference. Funnily enough, I came back more shaken. This is why:

A group of us delegates had gone out for dinner. As I got out of the car, a bullet whizzed past my head and knocked out a nearby store window - some hooligans were trying to rob the store. We quickly scuttled into the calm of the restaurant, thinking we'd be safe there. But no such luck. During the hour we spent in the restaurant, some miscreants entered it and stole from the cash register. Fortunately, we didn't actually see the theft take place as we were seated far away, but just knowing what was happening got us into a flap. We tried our best to stay calm, breathing deep as we traveled back to our hotel, only to find that my room had also been ransacked in our absence. That was the last straw. Deep breathing and every calm technique I could think of went straight out of the window - so much for thinking that I'd use the time out to collect my wits.

My room was a mess - I could hardly think of lying down and going off to sleep leaving it as it was... and to think that I had a speech to make at a session scheduled for early the next morning... it seemed impossible given my frame of mind. I decided that there was no point in even trying to go to sleep as I was too keyed up, it made more sense to stay up all night. I had a priest for company, he was also a delegate at the convention, and together, we downed one shot after another of scotch. The next morning, I somehow got through my speech and then finally went to bed. Thank God the economic situation in Ireland has improved since then, though what with the European Union bail-out and all happening as I write this, I'm not so sure things are genuinely better.

Anyway, I got back home, rattled by my experience yet still desperate for a chance to see things clearly and find the strength to take a stand. Fortunately, an opportunity came by soon after, though it happened in a rather unconventional manner.

Around that time, my gynecologist diagnosed fibroids in my abdomen and advised me to undergo a hysterectomy immediately. I got myself admitted to the hospital the very next day... told you, I'd do anything to get away.

During my week-long stay at the hospital, I woke up with a start one night - it was a now or never moment, a moment of reckoning. I decided to tell Larry that I was leaving him as soon as I got home. There was no question about it - I had to do it.

'I will not take any more nonsense.'

'I will stand up for myself.'

I went home with these inspiring words playing in my head, only to be tested a few hours later when Larry got provoked about something and made as though he was coming to strike me when he ordered my weak self (in mind and body) to get out of bed. That was it.

I moved downtown to a hotel for two weeks. Friends and acquaintances, bless them, thought that I had shifted there temporarily to be closer to my office and assisted me in every possible way. Of course, that wasn't the reason. I had to ask Larry for a divorce, but I needed to recover my strength for the battle that lay ahead.

I minced no words when I asked Larry for a divorce and made it clear that I wouldn't leave until he agreed. When I heard his response, I realized that the accountant in him had already done his calculations. Oh, he agreed to give me a divorce alright, but if (and only if), the girls continued to live with him. That was his last blow. It made the going very hard for me, but he wouldn't have it any other way. I felt sickened, not only because I knew I had to accept Larry's take-it-or-forget-about-a-divorce offer, but also because I felt really bad putting undue pressure on Jody. She was only eighteen at the time, though what with the goings-on in our household, she came across as more mature.

Looking back, I realize that the one thing that kept me going even when I knew that I'd no longer have the girls with me was the thought that they would probably be better off with Larry. They would continue to study in the same school with the same set of friends, besides which, at that point, Larry could offer them more comforts than I could have.

Over the next three months, I spent a lot of time talking to Larry about how we would split our belongings - equally. He could have the house, the chalet, furniture and so on. I'd take... But then I realized that we would have to go to court to execute a settlement, and what with Larry being a meticulous accountant and all, court proceedings would only prolong the saga and make the going that much harder for the kids. I decided that I would only take my clothes and five boxes of my personal belongings - nothing of any consequence whatsoever.

If you had to ask me now, I'd say that I was stupid not to take my half, even if it had meant going to court. A fairer split would have made my life much easier, plus the children, especially Jody, may have had an easier time if they'd got to spend more time with me. It's just that I was in such a hurry to get our divorce over and done with.

Deciding to opt-out of my marriage is one of the hardest choices I have ever made, even if it was inevitable. We couldn't possibly go on the same way, even though I hated the idea of our cherished dream coming to an end. Still, a divorce is a low that you think you'll never come out from. You need to be really inspired to go on, and usually, you're driven forward by the knowledge that there is no other way out. At least, that's how it was for me.

It was a time of my life when I took one day at a time, each day looking for signs that I'd made the right decision... and in many ways, I started again from scratch. I learned how to pay the bills and put gas in the car. I found a small place to live - a furnished apartment downtown. It was cheap because I had yet to sort out my finances. My new pad's interior echoed femininity in every nook and cranny - that's why I chose to call it The Pink Palace. I paid my first rent using my American Express card. I had no access to hard cash, as everything I had partially owned was in joint accounts that were now solely controlled by Larry. I also opened my first solo bank account since my marriage. I learned how to navigate my way through traffic and how to handle the kind of people you usually encounter downtown! Over the prior two decades of my life, I'd always visited the theatre downtown with Larry. Now, I struggled to cope alone. But slowly, very slowly, I grew more confident about performing day-to-day chores.

And seeing how my life has panned out after that, I'm so grateful I had the courage to walk out. To fast-forward to the present, Larry and I are now fine with each other. He married Audrey less than a year after our divorce, and she's been very good with Jody and Julie, thanks to which we share a good rapport. In fact, once Jody gifted Audrey and me a night away at an inn close to Toronto for Mother's Day - we each received gift vouchers that could be used anytime before the expiry date. Anyway, just by chance, Audrey and I booked on the same night. I can tell you we had a good laugh about it, so as they say, all's well that ends well.

I thank God that, like me, Larry has realized that there's no point being bitter when a relationship ends. Why not forgive each other for having changed? Why not accept responsibility for what you do, when it works out and even when it doesn't?

At this point in time, I am friends with a number of my exes. But I am bitter about none of them, not even about getting together and breaking up with two gentlemen about whom I have some reservations in my mind (complicated stories that will follow later). I think that's a positive state to be in, and I thank my pragmatic approach to life for my feeling this way. When I parted ways with my lovers, it was as though I reached a point where I still cared for them but realized that we were not suited to be together. In my mind, when you still care for a man but can no longer be with him, it makes sense to not storm out saying that you can't stand the sight of him, or clam up, or pick a fight to put an end to your relationship. No. It makes sense to move on with kindness.

EIGHTEEN

After the harrowing trauma of my divorce, I was desperate for some quiet time to heal. I didn't want to jump into another relationship too soon - the way I see it, that's just a way to mask your emotions and cover up what's going on inside. I also didn't want to run away from the fact that my marriage had broken up - I wanted to let that sink in and accept that we both had a role in our breakup. I also wanted to learn to enjoy my own company and experience that being alone doesn't necessarily mean being lonely.

A few months later, I came down from cloud serious, ready for some fun and romance, not necessarily without any strings attached. I think that somewhere in my mind, I was somewhat foolishly still looking for my white knight. Though I must confess that I hadn't given much thought to the sort of man I wanted to be with, and even when I started dating again, sooner rather than later, thanks to friends who took it upon themselves to set me up with men they found suitable for me, I didn't really sit back and analyze my dates. At first, that is.

Harvey was the first man I went out with after my marriage. My friend, the now late, Elizabeth, introduced me to him intending to show me the ropes (whatever that means). Allow me to describe Harvey - he was Jewish, handsome, separated from his wife, a great dresser, and a good dancer - I reckon he may have fit the image of the kind of man Elizabeth wanted to see me with. But he was so not the sort of man I wanted to be with, though it took me a couple of dates to learn about his shadier side. When Harvey told me that he sold swampland in Florida, I said, 'Great,' and when he told me that he took valium, I just smiled and said, 'OK'. You see, I had no idea what swampland was, nor did I see anything wrong with the valium part. That's how naïve I'd grown during my marriage. Larry had done a good job of sheltering me from many unpleasant facts of life. Then I figured out some more about Harvey and about swampland and valium and put two and two together, and that was the end of our twosome.

I met Tyler, or teddy bear Tyler, as I remember him, after parting ways with Harvey. Dating Tyler was like going out with someone from the next generation. He was tall (6'2" ish) and big-made (hence teddy bear) and twenty-two years younger than me though he acted as though he were about forty. A budding writer, he was well-read, that helped deceive some, and as for the rest, well, he had a beard which helped him look the part, a melodious voice and he was a veritable charmer of a man if there ever was one. I've always been a sucker for charming men, stupidly believing that dating is a 'what you see is what you get' kind of game, and therefore, a relationship with a man who comes across as charming on a first date is sure to end with an and-they-lived-happily-ever-after. That is so naïve, but there you are. That's me.

To come back to Tyler, I think I woke up to what I was doing during a date we had on my birthday. He turned up in a red panel truck (which should have warned me about the quirky evening that was to follow), presented me with a white corsage, and drove straight to Honest Ed's, an old-style Italian family restaurant, where we had a romantic candle-light dinner. Later that evening, when we got home, he played his favorite Beatles numbers so loud that we had the police come over to find out what the ruckus was all about. Was I embarrassed!... That's when I realized that however much I loved Tyler's exuberance (it reminded me of my youth), I couldn't kid myself about my age. I was at a stage where I wanted to enjoy the company of an interesting man who was somewhat more mature, not settle down with someone who had his entire life in front of him. Tyler was just starting out in life - he wanted a wife and lots of kids, and, let's face it, I couldn't help with that. So after two years of being together on and off, we called it quits. I genuinely wanted Tyler to settle down, and fortunately, he met and married Susan soon after we broke off, and they went on to have four kids to whom I am Aunt Betty.

So much for dating a younger man. Other men, older men, came into my life after Tyler but decidedly none 'qualified' as being my soul-mate, as indeed Shah Jahan must have experienced Mumtaz to have been his. I mean, it's common sense that you wouldn't build the Taj Mahal for someone you'd had a casual fling with. And looking up at the Taj Mahal, Shah Jahan's expression of his love for his departed wife, I wondered why soulmates don't necessarily live and grow old together. Life hadn't worked out that way for the emperor who'd lost his wife during childbirth. So even if and when my soulmate appeared, would he be around for the rest of my life? I sat on the bench, lost in thought until my guide came and yelled in my ear that I'd better be on my way.

NINETEEN

I returned to Delhi sometime in the afternoon, my mind tired from so much thinking and my body desperate for a long leisurely bubble bath to wash off the red dust I was covered in from head to toe. My flight back to Canada was at an unearthly hour that night, so I figured that I'd stay indoors and chill for the rest of the evening - order room service after my bath and pack. Little did I know then that once again, life was to show me that expectations fizzle out and that situations change almost instantaneously, hitting you like a bolt out of the blue.

This is what happened:

As I walked down the hallway to my room, planning my evening ahead, a man came running up the corridor yelling, "Is your TV working? I need something for a speech." I stood silly at the door of my now open room, without uttering another word, the man ran into my room, turned on the TV for about two minutes, and then ran out. All the while, I stood speechless, staring at him from the doorway. Sure, I made a mental note of the man's appearance - he was tall (at 6'2", he was really tall by Indian standards), very well dressed, elegant even. But I was dumbfounded. I couldn't bring myself to say anything. Even as he left, all I could do was shake my head and shut the door on him. Then I got busy with my plans.

Sometime later, the phone rang. It was the same gentleman. He apologized for his behavior and asked me out for a drink. I thought he merely wanted to appease his guilt for being rude and so refused, saying I had other plans for what was my last evening in India. When I put down the receiver, I felt smug, like I'd had the last word. But as it turned out, the gentleman was better prepared than I was. You see, he'd already thought out his Plan B.

About an hour on, there was a knock at my door. I opened it to see him, or rather, to see his face peeking through bunches of flowers. He gallantly presented me the flowers and suggested that he'd take me out to dinner and escort me to the airport after that.

I promptly accepted the invitation.

Huh?

Allow me to explain why I had a change of heart. Standing face to face with Jahangir, I knew.

What?

That something more was to come?

That he was a gentleman?

That I would never forgive myself for not accepting?

Well - maybe all of that, but there was something else that seemed far more important, and that was, I felt as though I'd known him all my life and that he knew me. I knew Jahangir, and he knew me - the feeling intrigued me.

Over dinner, I learned more about him, stuff that I hadn't known (by default) but which seemed so trivial to my knowing him. He was a politician representing a constituency in Bombay. He was also a lawyer and a judge. His Brazilian wife (I found that hard to digest but for some unfathomable reason took him at face value) had died in a car accident two years ago. He had a young son. And he lived with his father and son in Mumbai.

Jahangir kept his word (as I knew he would) and dropped me off at the airport after dinner. I felt so mad when I got through customs and found that my plane was delayed by six hours. If only I'd known I had more time, I could have gone on to a night club with Jahangir, or as he'd suggested, accepted his offer to have him escort me to the departure lounge where we could have chatted some more. If only...

TWENTY

As things stood, I thought I'd never see Jahangir again, which seemed such a pity, though, at the time, I wasn't quite sure why I felt that way.

I couldn't have been more wrong.

Close to twenty-four hours later, I reached home, completely exhausted by two long flights and a stop in London. When I settled in, out of habit, I pushed the playback button of my answering machine (presumably, to hear umpteen telephone messages from clients) and sat myself down on the couch, fiddling with the TV remote. I remember dropping the remote and running to the phone like a love-struck teenager when I heard Jahangir's voice ring through the room, saying, "I don't know who you are, but I would love to see you again and will arrange a visit to Toronto."

Wow. The message was as brief and as definite as that... It was such a pleasant surprise and completely unexpected, which made it so much more enjoyable. I played back the message again and again ('love-struck teenager,' I told you, didn't I?), and as I did so, I realized that Jahangir wasn't asking to meet me again. He was telling me we would. And he kept his word (as I knew he would).

A few weeks later, Jahangir left a second message on my answering machine. He'd called as unexpectedly as the first time; this time, he left me his travel dates, getting me into a flap. His message had said nothing about a hotel booking. Did that mean he wanted me to decide whether I wanted to put him up at a hotel or my house? To be on the safe side, I booked a suite in one of Toronto's best hotels, and when Jahangir arrived, I gave him the option of staying wherever he was more comfortable. He looked at me and said, 'My dear, I came halfway around the world to see you, not a hotel room'.

I was floored by his charm. I know this makes me sound naïve, but I always have been a sucker for romance.

So started my beautiful relationship with Jahangir, the only man I've ever felt for as a soulmate, and the only man I've felt had the same strength of character as my dad. Jahangir was a very special person with a great sense of purpose who was driven to work for the welfare of the poor. He was the kind of person who was pleased by the little things he did to make a difference in the lives of underprivileged people. Whenever he completed a village electrification project or had put toilets in a village, he'd call me to share his triumph - it was so cute. That is not to say he was any less ambitious about his political career. He'd say his goal in life was to be the President of India, no less. Thanks to my own interest in volunteering for politicians, I had great fun helping him plan his political campaigns. But I was amazed at the scale at which he campaigned - he made public speeches to eight to ten thousand people at a time, numbers we'd think were overwhelming for a rally in Canada.

When we spent time together, Jahangir and I talked about me becoming a greater part of his life, though after chatting some, we'd both laugh off the suggestion knowing that it wouldn't work - I had my life in Canada cut out and was not prepared to give it up (not even for a soul-mate), not that he ever asked me to. And we both knew that I wouldn't fit into his world, what with the social interactions his job entailed. If we had to go out for dinner, I'd feel ill at ease talking about parties, servants, or children in the ladies' room - I'd want to discuss politics with the men. But we kept up a long-distance relationship, chatting for hours on end every week, and meeting in India or Toronto every now and then.

TWENTY-ONE

My first visit to India proved to be far more eventful than I could ever have imagined. It had introduced me to the Brahma Kumaris and within it, many new friends, and of course, Jahangir. And I had more of Jahangir in my life in the weeks after I returned to Canada, and as it turned out, more of the Brahma Kumaris too.

Two months later, towards the end of 1990, I was invited to visit the Brahma Kumaris' Global Co-operation House in London, the largest center of the organization outside India, and at the time, also the place Dadi Janki operated from. I jumped at the opportunity to have daily one-on-one interactions about life with this amazing lady in a Western setting in which I'd feel more at home.

When we got into London, Dadi was up in Brighton for some garden party. Ant thought we shouldn't miss it, but strangely he didn't think he needed to tell me where we were going ('It's a surprise,' he said) until we were practically at the venue. When he finally told me, I squirmed in discomfort because I hadn't dressed for a Brahma Kumaris event. And it was too late to change my very short skirt.

We entered the garden, and Ant enthusiastically made a beeline for where the grand lady was sitting. I followed at a slower pace feeling so out of place and conscious of being the center of attention (that was bound to happen, no thanks to the way I was dressed). And then we were in front of Dadi, and the feeling only grew in intensity. She looked me up and down and up and down and then pursed her lips to show her disapproval.

I felt silly (schoolgirl silly, if there's such a phrase) and upset at the same time. I remember asking Ant, "Should she be noticing that, being spiritual and all?"

He just laughed.

I didn't need Ant to tell me that I hadn't got off to a good start, that much was obvious, but I hoped to patch things up with Dadi soon.

Moving on, I was put up in a lovely apartment near the Global Co-operation House when we got back to London. The interiors of the apartment reminded me of my stay in Mount Abu - the place was done up in every conceivable shade of white to denote cleanliness and purity, intended to help prepare guests for enlightening sessions with the Brahma Kumaris, in my case for conversations with Dadi Janki.

So we met - me in modest dress and all to get into the good books of this powerful lady who really intimidated me. And we chatted. And I asked Dadi all sorts of questions. And I appreciated her point of view about meditation and other stuff. But even by the end of a week's stay, I couldn't understand the need for a vegetarian diet or celibacy, both of which are lifestyle 'must-dos' for the Brahma Kumaris. In spite of that, I felt really close to Dadi Janki though I must admit I've never been able to figure out what she thinks about me.

To me, Dadi is street-smart, bright, kind, really sharp, tough as nails, and sometimes has little patience, but she makes up for that by genuinely caring for people. And yes, she tries to make the right decisions for the best of everyone - she's a great leader in that respect. Once, I was consulted by a CEO who wanted to create an office that people would be comfortable visiting to open their hearts and share their problems. I came up with the name The Person Office, and it went on to be very successful. That, to me, is the kind of leader Dadi is - a people's person.

I have great respect for her work ethic and how she responds to people - it's helped me develop a great connection with her. And I feel truly close to and respect my friends in the Brahma Kumaris too; they're people who've never asked me for money nor badgered me to be one of them. And in return, they fondly called me their 'associate' - it's a term that has stuck to this day.

TWENTY-TWO

I've just realized that I'm about one-third through my story and have only spoken about my maiden voyage to India, and within that, my frugal endeavors to understand spirituality and about the men in my life - no wonder someone suggested that this book should be about my lovers. Like that guy, you may have got the wrong impression about me too - that all I used to do was travel and romance men and no work to speak of at all.

Well, that's not true. When I left Larry, I had nothing of consequence whatsoever, and there was no question of asking for maintenance. So it was up to me to build my business to the point where it would afford me the luxuries life has to offer - such as travel. I worked, not every waking minute, as they say, but very hard, and was successful, far more successful than I'd ever thought I'd be.

My career was like a graph that starts at zero and zooms upwards to scale unexpected heights. It started in the tiniest, strangest way possible when one day around about when Jody was five, a volunteer came to our door with a letter for me to sign. I was a stay-at-home mom then and had all the time in the world to read the plea the guy was carrying around – not for pennies but for support to a move to fire the local school principal.

Curiosity got the better of me, and I attended the meeting only to find that the school was a mess. The elderly principal had all the kids calling teachers by their first names. One teacher doubled up as a nude artist in a late evening theatre show. Animals, beavers and ducks and what have you, had been let loose on the school premises. One parent thought of himself as some Guru and encouraged the kids to play around barefoot. It was a sorry state-of-affairs, and the thought that this was going to be my kids' school filled me with apprehension and dread. In a way, that also motivated me to help clean it up. I contacted the school board and thus began a career-long engagement with community affairs.

Larry was very supportive of my work. I think he was proud of the fact that I was helping society and doing something useful with my time.

Soon after, I was elected president of the Parents Association and started volunteering with Ratepayers groups and Children's Aid. I continued to be a hands-on mom, as best as I could manage, chairing meetings with one kid on each knee! I much preferred keeping the girls with me to hiring a babysitter, possibly because it lessened my guilt about leaving my kids behind and going off to work. Sometimes, my neighbors would look after the two just as I occasionally stepped in to look after their children.

All the work that I did at the start of my career was 100 percent community-oriented. My work with the Children's Aid, for instance, had me volunteering as a friendly visitor to three families. The plight of the first family made up of a very nice mother, a husband who didn't work, and five children opened my eyes to the extreme poverty that co-existed with seemingly boundless wealth in Toronto. Sure, I was aware of the upper, upper-middle, and middle-income class divides in the city, but I'd never been exposed to such abject hardship. They lived in a converted garage with minimal heating. One day, I walked in to find the mother beaming after a shopping trip inspired by the fact that she had enough money to buy pork chops. But the poor woman had stored her purchases on top of the hot water tank because she didn't know how to use her small fridge. I felt very sorry for her.

The second mother I interacted with would send her kids to the park with cigarettes to lure men home to have sex with her. I didn't last long with this family as I just couldn't bring myself round to working with the woman.

The third family was very large. As far as I recall, the couple had eight children. They were being evicted from their home, and I was sent in to help them resettle elsewhere. They had almost nothing by way of possessions – there wasn't a toy in the house, flimsy potato sacks draped the windows, it was nothing short of destitution. One day I had Jody with me, and when we got there, human feces lay just inside the door. Jody did this great big step over it, crinkling up her tiny nose in disgust. I felt sorry for her for having to see such squalid surroundings at such a young age, but at the same time, I found myself wondering what she'd have made of the situation.

Thank you, God, for looking after my family and me.

TWENTY-THREE

When you don't have a Godfather to show you the ropes of business nor sound qualifications to give you a leg up in advancing your career nor the useful exposure that private schooling gives you, it's up to you to make the most of the opportunities that come your way. The thing is, these openings aren't served hot on a platter - you sniff them out. Alternatively, you've got to be open to accept what life throws at you, however small the opportunity may seem, and try and make things happen with the limited resources you possess or can garner.

During my volunteering career, I never consciously looked out for ways to better my skills and get ahead, but I was always open to new ideas and to put myself in new situations. This openness helped me a great deal - it left me humble to learn my way through. When I found out that the local school had no playground for the children to play in, I was inspired to learn how to design creative children's playgrounds. Then I was inspired to apply for a grant to implement my newly gained knowledge. One thing followed the other. I really enjoyed seeing the creative playground I'd designed take shape. It wasn't as easy as it sounds, but my readiness to learn and willingness to ask for assistance in finding my way about helped.

From the looks of it, I'd 'arrived' as a 'community affairs' specialist. At least, I began to think so the day Larry pointed out, "You have all these professionals walking into this house asking for your advice..."

He left the latter part of the sentence unspoken - he didn't need to say more, his message came through loud and clear. Larry thought it was about time I started charging for the advice that I was by then dishing out on a regular basis. I'd like to believe that he meant well and genuinely felt that I was destined to move on to greener pastures. Besides, there was no denying that a second income would come in handy. It would allow us to travel and buy a weekend chalet in the country and so on. And to be honest, I was delighted because Larry's suggestive remark gave me the green signal to plunge into a more conventional career.

Nervous about applying for my first paid job, I decided to tread the shallow waters at first. I applied to the ministry of education for a grant of $12,000 to fund miscellaneous community development projects in a high-need area of Toronto. I reckoned that as my capabilities and skills had been tested in the area of school reform, it made sense to continue down the same avenue, so to speak. The job (if I got it) would require me to bring together formal groups representing educational associations and agencies that otherwise never shared information or interacted with each other. It sounds a bit boring put like that, but I thought it was cool, which shows how grateful I was for the opportunity to get out there and do something.

It was 1977. The grant came through and I went on to work long hours loving every bit of what I was doing. I chaired weekly people resource group meetings and had representatives of various agencies come together over a bag lunch at a local church. The participants would share information and pledge resources with the aim of solving all sorts of family and social issues. I honestly believe, if I say so myself, that the group that came together was the most effective community model I have ever seen.

We also had a contract to run the local Community Information Centre, during which I learned about other resources available to people across the province. And at one point, I chaired the Provincial Association of Community Information Centres.

Reading this chapter out loud, I realize that these achievements seem very small, perhaps even not worth sharing. The point is they were major steps forward in my career because I'd never imagined that I'd have a professional life, let alone get to be fairly well known in the community.

TWENTY-FOUR

Network, network, network. It's a mantra young execs are taught to follow from day one of their careers. 'Make the right contacts, if you want to get anywhere,' say experts. I never had the privilege to be taught that but learned the value of forming contacts as a matter of course. I don't feel bad about that because I know I'm the sort of person who learns best in 'live' settings. I don't think I would have made so much of classroom lectures.

As the years rolled on, I networked with a lot of prominent individuals and people from the corporate, government, education, and social service sectors (I built up four Rolodex lists over my career spanning twenty-three years, if that means anything). These contacts came in handy to push forward our community programs and to forge mutually beneficial relationships between disparate groups and individuals. I guess some of these acquaintances must have thought highly of my abilities too because when a vacancy for the post of executive director of a newly established community foundation of the Board of Education (called Community Outreach in Education or CORE) came up, they suggested that I apply.

Wow! That sounded exciting, like big things were happening in my life, but I was scared about taking on the job. I had no idea what to expect (an uncomfortable situation, to say the least) and if I could live up to their expectations (that left me feeling very nervous).

Anyway, I sought a meeting with (the now late) Karl Kinzinger, the director of the Board. Karl and I hit it off really well from the word go, but

I despondently thought it would take more than that for me to get the job.

I was right. They chose someone else, but I didn't get to know that until after I was offered the position. When they were doing a background reference check on the chosen one, they discovered that he'd squirreled away $100,000 of government funds. So the next best person got the job, that happened to be me (and there I was, thinking I was that impressive). When I heard all this, I reacted in a politically correct manner - I shook my head to show how appalled I was at the thought that someone could have done this sort of stuff - that was for the benefit of the guy who told me. Inside, I was jumping for joy, happy that things had worked out fine for me. But I also knew that I knew nothing, as the wise say, and that I needed to work doubly hard to keep the tempo in my favor.

The atmosphere in the Board of Education's head office was very political - so unlike the informal camaraderie infusing the people resource groups I'd chaired but an amazing learning experience all the same. And there was never a dull moment from the word go.

The purpose of the foundation was to raise funds for programs proposed to be run outside the school system for hard-to-serve children and young adults. My first project entailed convincing Shell Oil to donate a service station to the foundation, to be run by school students as a profit center to generate funds for other projects for their betterment. The first part of the project went off very well. My negotiations were successful - I still remember the president of Shell standing in the pouring rain to open the service station (no, he didn't complain at all, which was very kind of him).

The project ran very successfully for a few years until we grew wise to the fact that a school teacher was siphoning away some of the revenue. That came as a blow, not because I was accused in any way but because it took me all of six months to prove that the teacher (and not the students) had stolen the money.

I felt very protective about the students and was willing to do whatever it took to set the record straight. And it was really good that I felt so positively for the kids because a year on, I found myself fighting a battle against one of them since my own reputation was at stake.

Here's what had happened:

I'd taken up several unusual projects to enhance the public relations and image of the Board. One of these projects involved putting together a directory of community resources - we called it Key to North York. I hired twelve young adults to gather information for the directory - they were all bright kids. One boy, especially, I felt sorry for him because he was in a wheelchair. I wanted to give him a chance to prove his worth... which he did in a way that was entirely unbecoming of him - the young fellow accused me of sexually harassing him.

Ouch. I was furious (I could've killed him, the bum!). And the bombshell made it so embarrassing to talk to the other kids. But taking things personally wouldn't help. I had the full confidence of the offices of the director and a co-sponsor, and buried myself in paperwork to set things right - that meant writing to the government authorities who'd sanctioned the grant for the directory for permission to fire the boy. Which we finally did, and only then did I heave a sigh of relief.

TWENTY-FIVE

I made the most of the ample opportunities I had to network all through my five-year contract with CORE. I met up with loads of people, made great business contacts, and learned a lot about the community. Somewhere along the way, I was appointed Chair of the North York Business Association, where I met another special friend and mentor, Jim Peterson, a politician and member of a famous Canadian political family.

When my contract with the board ran out, I toyed with several possibilities. I could renew the contract, or take up a job with a corporation, or launch something on my own. They all seemed like great choices.

Unable to pick one, I asked a friend, Dr. Sy Eber, for his advice. Sy is a bright industrial sociologist who makes his living coaching the best business people in the country. He advised me never to work for anyone again and strike out on my own because he strongly believed that my temperament and caliber were best suited to run a business.

That's how my consulting firm Betty Steinhauer & Associates came into being, in 1983, to offer catalyst, facilitator, and advisory services (such as handling government relations, fundraising, marketing, strategic planning) to the public and private sector, and to forge relationships between business, education, not-for-profit and government organizations and/or individuals for their mutual advantage. Another mentor, (the now late) John Birnbaum, a public relations guy I knew as a friend of a friend, convinced me that my life would be easier if I worked as a consultant in return for a retainer fee. So that's what I did.

TWENTY-SIX

Armed with great advice, I set out to serve my first client - Xerox. I'd been hired by the executive vice-president to prepare a detailed summary and backgrounder of the new cabinet ministers in Ottawa. My mandate was to go beyond the ministers' bios to unearth information that would be useful for the government relations department of the company. Delighted to have Xerox as my first client, I pulled out all the stops in putting together the dossier. The contract was a major success and brought me more clients.

CORE contracted me to do some fund-raising, government lobbying, and marketing for them. It also fell upon me to improve the image of the director, my earlier colleague Karl, by spreading awareness of the role he played in the community. I chose to do this by creating opportunities for him to address and interact with the community. One of his first speeches was to members of the Women's Teachers Union. I'll never forget that night - it coincided with the time I'd undergone a hysterectomy and had moved downtown to get away from Larry. I attended the event dressed in a black suit so as not to stand out - the taxi driver who dropped me off called me 'a lady of the night.' That was cute!

I slipped inconspicuously in the last row at the venue. I figured that I'd be able to see how the speech came off sitting there and would also be protected from the fallout, if there were any - that was one of the advantages of being contracted to work but always stay in the background.

Karl was on a roll until he deviated from his well-rehearsed lines and emotionally proclaimed, 'Women can't go straight from the dishpan into management.'

Ooh. The audience went deathly quiet. 'Bad move,' I thought. Those were the days of women's lib so you can imagine the stir his words caused when the women in the gathering had digested his words - it was fun to watch from my vantage point, and we had a good laugh about it the next day.

My wide circle of friends and acquaintances brought me more work too. I remember my good friend, the late Kay Baxter, a diplomat representing Jamaica. I used to accompany Kay on her travels to Jamaica - it was great fun and gave me the chance to mingle with the government reps she had to meet. On one occasion, Edward Seaga, who was prime minister of Jamaica at the time, retained me to work out an arrangement whereby the Seventh Day Adventist church would be granted building permissions to construct more churches on the island in exchange for taking up a community project to benefit the inhabitants. It was a tricky assignment as the representatives of the church (from the head office in Washington) were very political and didn't like for a minute that they had to work with a woman. They tried everything possible to make my life difficult and prove that I wasn't good enough for the job, so I had to be one step ahead of them all the way, which made them madder.

It went on like that until the job was done. My client was happy as Jamaica got cheese and milk for all the school kids on the island for one year, and the Seventh Day Adventist church got what they wanted too. But we faced a strange last-minute snag - Jamaicans like canned rolled cheese and the Adventist group had sent cheddar cheese which no one would eat.

So I flew to Washington to meet more reps of the church... and finally, to cut a long story short, we got the right cheese.

And then, it was time for my treat!

I was all set to leave Jamaica the next day when a government guy came and told me that they had arranged a treat for me at a nearby hotel.

"It's a surprise," he said, his face beaming, making me wonder what it could be.

The car picked me up, and we drove to Negil, the location of the hotel. It was very dark when we arrived, I was exhausted and went straight to my room after checking in and hit the bed. The next morning, I woke up and pulled open the drapes... only to find to my greatest surprise that I was looking out onto a patio occupied by one man - who was nude except for the fact that he was wearing this huge gold watch (maybe the watch stood out more because it was the only thing he was wearing?). And my-my, there was more...

When I looked beyond, I saw that the patio gave way to the nude beach, which left me wondering - did my hosts really think that I'd strip and join the revelers? Or did they just think that I'd enjoy the sight?

Huh. So much for a Jamaican-style surprise treat... have I mentioned before that life sometimes springs surprises that aren't exactly what you'd choose? It helps to laugh off such moments, as I did that morning in Jamaica.

TWENTY-SEVEN

Over the years, I acquired some interesting nicknames at work - 'the can opener,' for one, for my effectiveness at pulling things off for clients. 'Orchestra leader' was another because they used to say, she's the one who pulls the strings. My forthright nature earned me the nickname 'straight shooter.' I believe I was good at what I did because I loved every minute I spent working.

Loving what you do for a living makes life so much more enjoyable because we spend so much of our time working. During the twenty-five years I worked as a consultant, I was always clued into my work. I made the most of technology to stay connected with my clients, even when we took family holidays. I understood that my clients might need me and I was always happy to do whatever it took to deliver the goods.

At one point, my business had grown so much that I thought of taking on a partner. So I interviewed a whole bunch of professionals, some of whom were really good at what they did and finally chose a lady. I thought she'd be the right fit and would bring shoals of experience to the business. And then, just before we were to sign a contract, she said to me, "I work hard, but I'm not willing to miss my two rounds of golf every week."

That was it. I knew at that instant that it wouldn't work. I needed a partner who thought like me. Who never tired of working simply because he or she was so grateful for the opportunity to do something he or she loved. And who was flexible about the balance between her personal and professional life. So I continued alone. In hindsight, I don't think that was the best decision - I should have continued looking for a partner. Taking on a second hand would have allowed me to take on more work. But more importantly, it would have given the business some continuity. As things stood, I was the business. The brand centered around me. That didn't give it a life beyond my working years.

For me, my career grew to be the single most important thing in my life. It's not as though my family and friends didn't matter. It's just that if I had to look back and pinpoint one aspect of my life that makes me feel good about myself, through and through, I'd have to say it's my work. My career was an unexpected pleasant surprise - it brought me colleagues who became lifelong friends, a wealth of experiences, and much success.

It's not as though my career came easy. No. I had confidence in my business instincts (they were spot on, which is a far cry from my instincts about men). It also helped that I slot myself into a one-of-a-kind niche by offering services that had no competitor. Most consultants would take on the sort of advisory work I did, backed by several legal experts - that put them into a different league altogether. I offered similar services for a lesser price, which helped further my business.

But even then, I spent sleepless nights worrying about whether the solutions I'd come up with would work. And that was the toughest part of my work: coming up with solutions. But it's funny, because the more I think about it, I realize that the best part about my work, the reason why opportunities came my way, was also my ability to spot the roadblocks, figure out a solution, and get the job done (my resume reads, 'What distinguishes Betty Steinhauer... a solid record of 'getting it done''). To me, that suggests that if life throws you a challenging opportunity, it also gives you the skills to pull yourself out of the situation. At least, that's how my life turned out. And along the way, I also looked for ways to improve my abilities. Travel was one of these means - putting myself out there, in out-of-the-way areas helped sharpen my survival instincts. It also deepened my understanding of people. Both of these skills helped me run my business successfully.

TWENTY-EIGHT

So. I hope I've made the point that I had a business to run and was working hard to steer it forward. In 1991, I was also doing a lot of work for the directors of education across Canada, helping them develop new relationships with organizations and corporations outside of education to see where the new partnerships could take them.

I worked hard and partied hard and holiday-ed well, which usually meant traveling to offbeat places. Such as, also in 1991, twelve wealthy Canadians (our group included the late Tom Bata, president of Bata Shoes) and a poor church mouse (me) were asked to visit Costa Rica on behalf of the Canadian Wildlife Fund, to check out some environmental hotspots and report whether the country's tourist circuit was up to speed.

San Jose, the capital, was pathetic. We saw people doing drugs and prostitutes all over the place. That made me realize just how poor the country was.

Then we moved on to the Tortuguero National Park, which was much better. The park was located in a jungle bordering the seashore. I counted myself as the luckiest of the group for having the best hotel accommodation ever in that Godforsaken spot – a hammock filled with down cushions on the beach.

'That'll be fun,' I thought when I saw my bed and had a lovely vision of myself lolling in bed watching the sun rise... until I was told to banish any thoughts I had of sleeping-in because we had to get up religiously at four in the morning (every morning, yuck) to track a certain bird (the quetzal).

We walked and walked, through rain forests at that, which is neither easy nor pleasant, but to no avail. The elusive bird ensured that it stayed out of our sight. Fortunately, other spectacles made up for the lack of spotting our target. Tom was writing a book at the time, and it was amusing to see him jot down the bright ideas that came to him on his hand as we walked. But the weather in rain forests changes by the minute. The rain would come down without any warning (fortunately, rain in rain forests feels like a gentle warm spring shower) as we walked and wash off his writing.

This trip also marked my first attempt at giving up smoking. The sanctity of the pristine surroundings we stayed in made me feel really bad about smoking. I think when you spend time close to nature, you come nearer to your better side, your unspoiled self. Walking through those rain forests, I realized just how far I'd come from living naturally... and I felt ashamed. I thought of quitting. But as every chain-smoker knows, thinking of quitting is much, much easier than actually doing so... until one night at dinner, I found this statue of a skull and crossbones at my place with a note saying, 'This could be you.' (Courtesy Tom, only the note didn't say that.)

That gave me the heebie-jeebies. I stopped smoking for the rest of the trip, which was a start... it took me all of the next eight years to give up for good.

TWENTY-NINE

"I want to meet your girls," said Jahangir, taking me completely by surprise (he had this strange ability to do so). We'd been chatting about the highlights of my Costa Rica trip when he suddenly came up with that request. I couldn't refuse, and as he was visiting me the week after, I got onto Jody and Julie straight away.

I was nervous about introducing Jahangir to the girls. Not that I wanted him to remain the mystery-man-in-India-who-mother-loves to them, it's just that I wasn't sure how they'd take to him, especially Jody.

Jody, my eldest, and I have had a difficult relationship, which is sad in some ways because she's a very successful person in her own right. She was good academically, the kind of kid who makes efforts to be independent. I remember how pleased she was when she signed up for a magazine route when she was in her teens because it meant she'd earn her own pocket money. Jody was always outgoing, attractive, a good dresser, and not surprisingly, very popular with boys (and there was I, wanting to put her and Julie for that matter on the pill, just in case, because I couldn't keep tabs on what they were up to).

Jody grew closer to her father when she was in her mid-teens for the simple reason that the kids could get away with much more with him. Larry and my relationship had taken a turn for the worse by then, as a result of which we didn't come together as parents and take a joint firm stand on things. I refused to pamper the girls because I wanted them to learn that life isn't a bed of roses, whereas Larry wanted to be seen as the more indulgent parent and make me out to be the bad one. It was our mistake - we created a situation the girls could take advantage of, and they did.

Matters between Jody and I got worse in the months following our divorce. Initially, I tried to split their weekdays so that Jody and Julie could spend time with me. But it wasn't easy. Larry had insisted that the girls stay with him - that was his main condition for giving me a divorce, and I guess in the immediate aftermath of my moving away, before Larry remarried, a lot of the housework fell on Jody, being the eldest. Putting her in that situation really hurt me, especially as there was nothing I could do to help her. I know I should have comforted her, but at the time, I was emotionally drained and nothing short of a nervous wreck. How could I be a pillar of support to my girls when I was barely getting by myself? Jody reacted by drawing away from me - she stopped talking to me, blaming me for the hardships that came her way.

It was hard going. I tried sending her cards and gifts by mail and sometimes dropped parcels by the house, but she didn't reply. It seemed almost impossible to reach out to her. This impasse went on for a good two years until she called me late one night and talked and talked as I listened, willing myself to keep quiet to let her vent her feelings. There would be enough time to explain my viewpoint later, if we patched things up. And getting our relationship back on track was more important to me.

It took years, but slowly, we bridged the distance that had grown between us, as she learned to respect my views and needs, and I, hers. It's not as though our relationship became easy - it was still difficult in parts. Even today, I find myself biting my tongue every now and then. But things are more manageable. And our relationship improved some more after my grandchildren came along. Jody is a good mother and really works hard to live a good life. Once, she actually said that I was the best grandparent. Boy - was I surprised to hear that!

THIRTY

Jahangir and I went over to Jody's place for coffee. He was his usual charming self and presented her a bracelet he'd brought for her from India. But the meeting was a disaster. Oh, Jody was polite but so uptight and uncomfortable it showed. I couldn't fathom what the matter was with her. I mean, I didn't expect her to be any more than civil and attentive. But she refused to speak more than monosyllables, and that made it difficult to hold a regular conversation. I was so embarrassed. Needless to say, we left very soon.

When I spoke to her on the phone the next day, she made the comment that all Indians smell. I was upset - Jahangir didn't smell except for cologne. I hadn't realized she had such a mental block for people from non-white backgrounds (she didn't get that attitude from her mother for sure).

My telephone conversation with Jody made me so apprehensive - we were meeting Julie for dinner later the same day, and I wondered if I was letting ourselves in for another disastrous encounter. But I needn't have worried. Julie, my free spirit, didn't let me down at all.

Julie, bless her, came into my life as a breath of fresh air. She's carefree through and through and was like that from the word go when Larry and I adopted her soon after Terri died. That's one of the reasons why I call her my free spirit. I also think I grew more outgoing after she came into our lives.

Larry and I decided to adopt a little girl because we were afraid that another child might be born with the same problem as Terri. So we applied to Children's Aid and were lucky as just three months later, a baby girl came up for adoption. One of her parents was a Jewish doctor, and since we were the only Jewish family on the list, she came to us.

Julie Dana, as we called her, came to us looking like a doll in a store window display, in a pretty long pink dress. Well, that was the last time she looked like that. Though she was only three months old when she entered our lives, it took Julie just a few days to show us that she'd bring us a wealth of new experiences, carefree experiences at that. She was a very busy baby with absolutely no time for naps, busy from the word go, with an amazing ability to make fun of supposedly serious situations. She'd throw up at meals and then look at us with a big smile on her face, as though saying, 'So?'

We took Julie for a check-up one month after she'd been with us. It was a routine examination as her health had given us no cause for concern. So imagine our shock when the pediatrician told us he heard heart murmurs. I just wanted to die.

THIRTY-ONE

Waves of emotion engulfed me. I just couldn't bring myself around to feeling optimistic about the way ahead. I feared the worst. And yet, I pleaded in my mind, to a random God above. 'Please, no, not again. Let nothing bad happen to Julie.'

I just couldn't face another ordeal like that.

Off we went to the Sick Children's Hospital for many tests. Seeing babies being poked and prodded is torture for any parent, and there we were, going through it all over again, not knowing whether Julie would come out of it alive. I would stand there watching and thinking life is so unfair.

Doctors discovered that Julie had an open valve in her heart and would need surgery. They said this surgery was routinely performed for many infants with the same condition, so we had nothing to fear.

But you know doctors, they offer no guarantees. The surgeon said, "The operation will in all likelihood be a success, and Julie will recover well."

Until today, I don't like the words 'in all likelihood.' I like a firm yes or no - it's easier on the system.

Besides, there was a catch - of course, there had to be. We'd have to wait until Julie was eleven months old to have her operated on.

Those months, watching Julie grow in loveliness and naughtiness, yet with the specter of heart surgery looming over her all the while, were one of the toughest periods of my life. The question, 'Why us?' played over and over in my mind. It was a thought that had first entered my mind when Terri died; only then, I'd reflected more on the lines of 'Why Terri?'

Our social worker was beside herself when we found out about Julie, though she tried to make sense of it all, saying that she was so sorry, but Julie had the best parents because we had been through a similar situation with Terri.

I could only manage a weak smile in response.

Why us?

Why us?

Why us?

I couldn't get that off my mind.

THIRTY-TWO

In adopting Julie, Larry and I had sought to fulfill more than our desire for a second child. We'd also wanted to bridge the differences between us that were slowly coming to light. We couldn't comfort each other after Terri, and we thought maybe another child would bring the family together again.

But problems have a funny way of reappearing. Try to run away from an unresolved issue, and the odds are, it'll come back to haunt you.

Once more, we faced moments of doubt. Were we doing the best for Julie? And for a second time, we resorted to our own methods to face these issues, and as these were as similar as black and white, we slowly drifted further apart.

I tried to spend as much time as I could with Jody. Losing Terri had been hard on her as well - she was too young to understand but not too young to not feel, which is a horrible situation to be in. I didn't want her to think that she was going to lose a sister again.

I don't remember which of us reacted most intensely when we heard that Julie's surgery had gone off well and that she'd be okay. We had so much emotion pent up inside us! But it was true - our dark night was finally coming to an end. Julie spent a week in the ICU and was then declared to be out of the woods.

I can still relive the moments when, lying in the ICU, my busy little baby kept trying to pull out all the tubes sticking in her body. The nurses were so disturbed they'd kept a round-the-clock watch on her, and they just couldn't figure out why Julie's 'activities' brought a huge smile of relief and happiness to my face. I thought it was great - she was alive and kicking.

Julie's mischief continued after she was transferred to the children's ward. During one visit, I recollect Julie was nowhere to be found. After a frantic search, she was found in her walker, in a linen closet pulling all the sheets over her head, having a whale of a time.

Fifty years later, Julie still has a scar that we fondly call her 'zipper.' And she's set a record of sorts for being carefree at every stage of her life.

When Julie was in school, she made it amply clear that she hated studying and would often say that she didn't feel the need for formal education. Needless to say, her school records were a disaster. When Julie entered her teens, she asked if she could visit Hawaii instead of having her Bat Mitzvah - a Jewish religious ceremony - as Jody had had.

Julie tried taking some courses at a Community College, but it didn't work. She'd be all over the place instead of being where she should've been - in the classroom. But Julie was easier to relate to during my divorce. She was sad when I left home and openly expressed her feelings in an essay I have treasured all these years. For all her wild ways, Julie was an amazingly perceptive youngster - her words left me in no doubt that she understood what was going through my mind and the reasons that had driven me away.

Adsignment #1
For: Jon Sudlow
Submitted by: Juli Steinhauer WYL 207
Audience: Mr.Jon Sudlow
Purpose: To prove who is the greatest influence in my life and who I would want to be.
Role: Daughter proud of who her mom is.

There I stood watching a mother beating the living
hell out of her kid in Food City.
I was in the produce section, holding my oranges with
my mouth wide open in disbeleif.
I knew right then and there how lucky I was to have a mother
like Betty Steinhauer.
My mom had a tragic life from almost the beginning.
Her father died of a sudden heart attack when she was just
15 years old, leaving her and her mother alone.
She then had to grow up fast. She quit scool and got a full
time job.
She stood still, watching her friends move on to proms, boy
friends and college, where she should have been.
Her mother also suffered from mental and physical illness,
which just made the burden that much heavier.
She was only a child herself and had all these responibilit-
ies of an adult expected of her.
It hardly seemed fair for a girl so young.
However, things began to take a positive turn when she
met and married my father.
He came form a wealthy and well eduacated family who she
now had a chance to become part of,
The fact that he was Jewish and she was not was never truly
accepted by his family,
The fact that she later converted to please his family was
still not enough for them.
Shortly after her marriage, her mother was diagnosed with
Cancer.
Later in 1976, she had to pull the life support system, the
-re she was in her thirties and already an orphan.
This was very tramatic to lose her parents but also to lose
her, childrens' grandparents,
Some time later in 1986, she and my dad were divorced.
At that time she had to make the choice of leaving her 2
daughters in the custody of her husband.
The decision was finally made to disolve a loveless marriage
se for the sake of her family.
Knowing this was the best decision for everyone involved,
my mom left and went out on her own.
I still remember standing in the driveway watching my mom
pull away in her car with tears streaming down my face.
My moms' concentrations then moved into opening her own
Consulting Firm.
She put a lot of time and dedication into launching her new
business while trying to still be my mother.
This was a hard balance to acheive, however, she did it with
with all the care and grace I knew she could.

Finally, when her business became very sucessful
she threw a big party.
I remember standing there among the honoured guests
feeling so proud to be her daughter.
She made it clear how happy she was in her own life and
how glad she was that I could be a part of it.
There was a sense of warmth in peoples eyes when I was
introduced as Bettys' daughter.
I felt like everything had finally come together for her,
after a life of struggling, hapiness and sucess was all hers,
I knew it could be done, right then and there that life was
what you made it.
There was my mom, in all her glory, while only a few
people knew what she had to do to get there.
To this day, my mom has been the greatest influence in my
life, and I would do it the way she did with setermination
I admire many of her qualities especially being able to
beat the odds and make something out of herself.
When I feel sometimes like giving up, I think of her as my
inspiration.
My mom, my friend, the one who can always make me smile.

Belted -- Be aware of your structure

-- Develop each idea in 4 to 6 sentences.

li's = he is

She's grown up to be one of the most carefree adults I've ever seen. She's just as into doing her own thing now, at fifty. She doesn't plan for her future at all. She has no money in the bank, no security, and is only starting to think about that stuff. She is also very naïve about men (I think she gets that from her mother). And she couldn't be more different from Jody to look at. Julie's a pretty woman - small-made with a great figure, and she lights up every room she walks into. She's totally into looks - hair color (which she changes like other girls change clothes), makeup and perfumes (of which she has the largest collection that I have ever seen).

And she was so much more pleasant to introduce Jahangir to. We all had dinner, and she was taken in by his charm (like her mother) and really liked him. And Jahangir appreciated the honesty in our relationship and that Julie knew that she was adopted. In fact, Julie told him how we'd read a storybook about adoption to her once a week when she was a kid.

"You should be proud of your girls," he said as he was leaving. I was so happy. That felt good.

THIRTY-THREE

I had one affair during my marriage, with Peter. There. I knew that had to come in someplace, and it had to be here. Because I'm talking about the year 1992 now, and it was during that year when, one day, I was driving to work when I received a call from Peter.

We hadn't spoken in ages, so I was really surprised to hear from him, and even more so when he asked me to pull over, which I did. Then he told me he had cancer and was going to die.

I drove right over to his mansion, where I found him sitting in his large library. The Peter I remembered was single, good-looking (he had the most appealing beard that added to his charm), dapper, and every inch a man about town. Women loved him, me too. But now he'd lost so much weight he looked awful. I felt so helpless sitting there, shamelessly crying my heart out for the dying man sitting in front of me.

Peter and I met in the later years of my married life when we worked together on an election campaign. Working in election campaigns is something I started doing during my volunteering years and continued to do even after I got really busy with my professional career - I felt I needed to do this to fulfill a social responsibility. Besides, campaigns were great places to make new contacts. I worked for politician Jim Peterson's campaign too.

Coming back to Peter, he was ten years older than me and lived with his mother in a mansion that was frequented by the veritable who's who of the political arena in Toronto. And, he drove a jeep. As far as I was concerned, that made him the last word in style.

I got to know Peter very well during the campaign and must admit that I really liked him and enjoyed learning more about politics and the process of elections from him. It didn't matter that he was working for the Tory's and I for the Liberals.

In retrospect, I'd say that he was the perfect guy to have an affair with, not that that gave me an excuse, but whatever. Peter was interesting to talk to and lots of fun. More importantly, he really cared about me as a person. I loved that, since by then, I really craved attention. I know that sounds pathetic, but it is exactly what life had reduced me to, or to not gratify my feelings, what I had let life make of me.

We wormed our way into each others' lives and affections over the ensuing months. But to be true to my marriage vows, I ruled out any further involvement. 'I am a married woman,' 'I can't betray Larry,' 'How can I possibly have an affair' - I couldn't quite get such thoughts out of my head. So although we were attracted to each other, we didn't act upon the impulse. At first, that is.

The inevitable was bound to happen. Larry and I had been unable to comfort ourselves during our episodes with Terri and Julie, and now that we were coming from different places, we were also no longer fulfilling our sexual needs. We'd had no intimacy for a long time, and all my successes at work were not enough to fill the void that consequently developed within.

It was funny - on the one hand, I desperately needed to feel wanted. On the other, I felt overwhelmed with guilt when I started going out with Peter. As a result, we didn't go to bed for about five months, by which time Peter used to tell me that he thought he'd lost it! Fortunately (for him and on second thoughts, for me too), we both attended a political meeting in Ottawa, and it was there, away from the stresses of my life in Toronto that Peter and I first slept together.

THIRTY-FOUR

I look back on my relationship with Peter with the utmost fondness. You know how it feels like to be well looked after? Well, that was the feeling that first came to my mind when we started going out. I also experienced other emotions that I'd ignored during the years my marriage soured. I had been an extrovert in my youth, but my marriage troubles had turned me into a quieter person. In Peter's company, I felt myself relaxing, and once again, enjoying the good things that life has to offer. Peter taught me so much, not only about politics but how to read people and how important it is to live in the present moment to make the most of life.

Peter was given to putting up a brave face in public – he'd utter his pet phrase 'damn the torpedoes' whenever he faced a situation the upshot of which might be unpleasant. But I recognized his external façade for what it was. I knew that though he acted as if he didn't care about what he did or what people said, Peter was always concerned, big time. Perhaps that is why about seven months on, Peter broke off our affair. He'd always thought of himself as a confirmed bachelor, so it unnerved him that he was becoming emotionally involved with a woman, a married woman at that. Who, according to him, was screwed up and seriously needed to sit back and think about her life. He was right. Having an affair had brought me momentary happiness, but it hadn't solved anything at home. So in a sense, I owed Peter a huge debt for helping me think about getting a divorce from

Larry.

Peter spent his last days in a country hospital where he was put on experimental drugs. I paid him many visits, accompanied by a mutual friend of ours, braving snowstorms to reach. Not that that mattered, Peter had given me so much. It was payback time now. I wanted to be there for him when he needed me the most. Only I didn't have much time.

One day, barely a few months after we'd reconnected, he called me saying that he was going home. Of course he wasn't. It was the drugs talking. Peter died later the same day.

I'll never forget his funeral, packed with anyone worth their salt in Toronto, not because they had to show their faces but because of Peter. That was the kind of man he was, I was glad to have been so close to him.

THIRTY-FIVE

Towards the end of 1992, I had the urge to travel to India again. I'd stop-over in Mumbai, then get to Mount Abu somehow (yes, that same place I'd freaked out in, and also the place where I'd made such good friends and spoken so openly and resolutely with God), and then tour the country some. I seemed to have developed a strange fascination for Mount Abu, and within it, the Brahma Kumaris, who would once again be my hosts.

But first, there was Mumbai and Jahangir to look forward to. It had been a tough year for Jahangir - India's dynamic young prime minister, and his good friend Rajiv Gandhi had been assassinated just months earlier. Jahangir was beside himself when that happened. And I was worried sick when it happened. Jahangir was supposed to have been with Gandhi, on the same stage, when the young prime minister was assassinated. But a last-minute change in the arrangements had taken him elsewhere. I didn't know that and spent three worrisome days scouring newspapers for the names of the other people who'd also died with Gandhi. Then finally, he called, and I was so relieved to hear his voice and know that he was alive.

Jahangir had known Gandhi from his student days at Cambridge and Oxford - apparently, they'd been roommates. When we first spoke over the phone after Gandhi's death, Jahangir told me that he now wanted to get more involved with politics and especially help Sonia Gandhi, the slain leader's widow, find her feet in the Indian political scenario.

Mumbai turned out to be a non-starter. Jahangir and I had got our dates mixed up - he was away on a political campaign when I called him after my flight landed, and though he made a mad rush to get to Mumbai to meet me, it was touch and go - a short and sweet meeting. I invited him to Mount Abu, thinking the break would be good for him (and we'd get to spend more time together) but he wouldn't have any of that - he'd heard about the Brahma Kumaris from Gandhi and didn't like the sound of them (celibacy freaked him out). So I flew to Ahmedabad and traveled by road to the mountain top (alone, and far more confidently than my first time).

THIRTY-SIX

My second visit to Mount Abu was as eventful as my first, though for entirely different reasons. It was colder up on the mountain this time, much colder, and I was unprepared. Less than twenty-four hours into my stay, before I could even think of buying a sweater from the local market, I caught a cold. 'It's nothing that cups of steaming tea from the chai kitchen can't cure,' I reckoned. But things worked out differently.

My cold rapidly got worse, before I knew it, I was laid up with pneumonia. In another first, of an entirely different kind though, I ended up as the first Western patient to be admitted to the J Watumull Global Hospital and Research Centre, a hospital established by the Brahma Kumaris barely three kilometers from 'the abode of bliss', the building I'd been put up in for a second time.

I don't quite remember the hospital admission process - it all happened so fast, and before I grasped what was going on, I found myself being wheeled into an operating room. Ouch. For the love of God, why? Whoever heard of surgery for pneumonia? It made no sense.

I panicked, seeing nurses wearing sterile green gowns approach me, and somehow managed a stern, "No operation," hoping against hope that at least one spoke English?

One did, thank God, she was the supervisor, and she told me that I'd only been transferred to the operating room because I'd be more comfortable there (I'm still not sure why they thought I'd be better off lying in the operating room instead of a ward room, maybe because the place was air-conditioned?).

Duh.

The supervisor's words made no sense - I felt only slightly mollified. On top of that, the theatre had this eerie oval-shaped red light fitted to one of its walls, which scared me out of my wits. Fortunately, sweet (in this case) exhaustion got the better of me, and I remember flopping back on the bed and dozing off.

Over the next few days, the nurses were in and out of my room every so often, and that wasn't all. It is the custom in India for a hospital patient to be accompanied by an attendant (who is usually a relative). Since I was alone, I had two attendants ordered to sit at my bedside 24x7. These two ancient-looking women, who took turns to sit at the end of my bed with a steam vapor machine, were fascinating. Every half hour or so, they'd urge me to use the machine, pointing at it and then to me - it was all very suggestive. I must have been asked to take steam about eleventy-six times during the seven days I was in the hospital. A great one for not taking suggestions that I am, I pretended to be asleep most of the time, just to get out of the steam routine.

But they say you should give credit when it is due, so I hereby place it on record that the steam machine may have precipitated my recovery. Or perhaps it was the help offered by (the now late) Dr. Vinay Laxmi, an Indian doctor trained in the UK, who was kind enough to make soup for me in her quarters every evening as I found the hospital meals hard to digest? I'll always be grateful for that.

I must also share this: when I got back home about two weeks later, a FedEx parcel arrived out of the blue. It contained every single slip of paper relating to my hospital stay - mentioning treatments I had received, medications I had taken, my diet during my stay in the hospital, and my x-rays. I hadn't asked for all this to be sent but was impressed all the same. I sent the hospital a donation, a small expression of my gratitude.

Coming back to my story, when I was better, I was curious to know more about the hospital that had been commissioned barely a year prior to my visit. It hadn't been around when I'd visited in 1990, and I was keen to know why the Brahma Kumaris had ventured into healthcare.

I learned that the hospital project had been seen as a means to plug the gaping holes in healthcare in the area. Four hospitals having 457 beds between them served the district population of 700,000. That sounded too low by any standards. And I wasn't surprised to learn that though it was still in its infancy, so to speak, the Brahma Kumaris' hospital had already launched a village outreach program to deliver healthcare to people living in remote villages at their doorstep. In spite of the grim ground realities, it sounded like they were doing a good job.

I also learned that the hospital was always on the lookout for funding for community projects that would improve lives in these far-flung villages. This was a subject that interested me no end, coming from where I did. The idea that for only about $1000 or so, you can bore a well for an entire village to avail water or supply the same people with enough penicillin to cure common sicknesses occurring over the course of a year, roused my interest and I asked to visit a village.

The visit was an eye-opener and an emotional roller-coaster for me. Dr. Vinay Laxmi, the head of the program, and I traveled for what seemed like forever, through dusty narrow lanes to reach the first of the six villages we were to visit. As the bus approached the settlement, I saw many women carrying infants or holding hands of children, old women, and men, and all sorts of diseased people following it as the driver slowly steered the vehicle forward and parked. Then they hovered around the bus waiting for the doctor to get out. And when she appeared in the doorway, the crowd almost mobbed her, desperate to get her attention. It was the same story wherever we went. The extent of deprivation of these people caught me completely by surprise - it was a shock to the system. But it was nothing compared to the sense of deja vu that followed.

THIRTY-SEVEN

As the doctor wound up her work in what she said was our last stop, she was approached by some people who consulted her about something. I didn't understand a word they said (obviously) but noted that none of them seemed sick. Maybe they were asking her to visit a patient at home? She gave them some instructions, though shaking her head and looking decidedly unhappy with what she'd just heard. Then she walked away and motioned me to follow.

I looked at her questioningly as we walked back to the bus. The bus was parked on the outskirts of the village. As we reached it, she pointed out a shack in the distance and said, "There's a young man locked in there."

My 'Why' was answered by, "Because he has a mental illness, which these people don't understand. They think that he's been attacked by an evil spirit and is safer put away."

"Goodness."

And then, as a wave of thoughts engulfed my mind, "But do they let him out sometime? Do they feed him? For how long will he stay locked up?"...

These were just a few of the questions that I felt desperate to know the answers to.

Yes, desperate. At that point, the 'desperate' in my reaction seemed to be more pronounced than that in the villagers' response to the 'abnormal' one among them. It took the doctor by surprise, and she looked at me rather pitifully, thinking I was upset only about the 'treatment' being given to the young man.

"Not quite the way he'd be treated in the developed world, is it?"

I shook my head and climbed onto the bus.

The view outside the window, of villagers diligently working in green fields, absorbed me as we pulled away. They were simple folk - precious few of them had studied beyond the age of ten. So it wasn't surprising that they believed in the Indian equivalent of witchcraft instead of modern medicine that would at least have allowed the patient to live freely. But that wasn't what upset me the most. I felt worse for the young man, for what he had to endure because I'm of the firm belief that even in their sickness, mental patients know what is happening to them. And it's not like my belief stems from imagination. No. It comes from my firsthand experiences with a mental patient who was very close to me, who lived in the same house as me - my mother.

THIRTY-EIGHT

Many years ago, around about when I was in my late teens, Mom finally gave way. I say finally because it had been building up for so many years. I'd seen her sick for most of my childhood, but after Dad died, she went downhill even faster. In retrospect, I'd say that the quietness that was part of her persona during the years Dad was alive showed that she had a problem then too. I now realize that Dad understood the working of her mind probably better than she did herself - that's why he encouraged me to stand on my own feet and make my own decisions from a young age.

Outwardly, Mom gave you the impression that she was calm, but I don't think her mind was tranquil - it's just that Dad protected her so much that she never had to exert herself, and as a result, we never got to see her agitated, as long as he was around, that is. She was completely dependent on her husband, so much so that she had no other friends to speak of. That's why Mother was very, very lonely after he died. If she was reserved before, she sort of clammed up after he passed away - to the point where it was hard to get a word out of her. I think Dad's going was the last straw, the loss of her backbone. That, coupled with her poor general health, may have led Mom to believe that she had nothing more to look forward to in life.

One day, I came home from work to find her talking to herself, saying that she was Judas at the Last Supper. I watched her, aghast at what was going on - she walked into the kitchen, took a knife out of the drawer, and threw it at me. I dodged, but only just.

Sure, I realized that something was seriously wrong, but I had no idea what to do to make things better for her. My friend John (I think of him as John Travolta now because he was cute in a similar way, he had slicked-back hair with a little curl) wanted to come in and help, but Mom wouldn't let anyone enter our apartment. So he stayed on call; sleeping on the floor of the lobby of our apartment for two nights while inside, I couldn't sleep for fear of what Mother would do. This sorry state of affairs went on for three days.

Until finally, I realized that there was no way out but to call for professional help - the doctor who came in diagnosed her illness as schizophrenia. He said she needed to be taken to the mental hospital on Queen Street, but we needed two doctors to commit her. It took us two more days to arrange this. Then, on the third day, I took her to the hospital, all the while hating myself for doing so, but not because she was my mother and had done so much for me that I wanted to give back. No. We'd never grown close that way. In fact, it wasn't until after I became a mother that I grew aware of just how distant we'd been - I realized that the lack of involved mothering in my own life led me to sometimes feel at a loss when handling my own children. I used to watch other mothers - mothering came naturally to them but not to me. I often used to wonder about what mothering was actually all about... much of my mothering was making sure that everything was done - the house was clean and the kids had everything they needed, but was that enough? Did that make me a good mother? I don't know... Today, I realize that Mom hadn't been much of a role model for me to follow... Nor had I had a granny around when I was growing up, and that may have meant that my kids didn't get the best mothering.

Still, I felt desperately sorry for Mom when she was going through her worst hour. She deserved better. Every human deserves better than living in a mental hospital. You just have to visit one to feel that way.

I grew to be an informal volunteer advocate for the mental patients during the years that Mother spent in the hospital. I'd complain whenever I saw a patient being abused or treated less than ideally. This went on for about two years until the executive director quit. I think he grew tired of me, the young lady who was always complaining about the way the place was run. Years later, when I was on the Board of a mental health organization, I interviewed the same gentleman for a consulting position. He kept looking at me as though I reminded him of someone. Finally, he asked, "Have we met before?" I said yes, and told him my maiden name. You should've seen his face fall - he knew that there was no way he'd get the job.

Coming back to Mother, I knew that my hands were tied - I couldn't get through to her, to help her. So I had to rely on the mental hospital for what it was worth.

Admitting Mom to the hospital was the start of a cycle that lasted many years. She'd stay in the hospital for one month, and then be sent home for a few months, with the intention of encouraging her to manage herself with the help of pills. Every time she came home, I hoped that it would be forever... again, not because we were close, but as I said, just so that she wouldn't have to go back to that wretched hospital. I hated it. And I hated it more when she'd break down at home and have to be readmitted sooner than expected.

Other times, she'd fool the hospital guards and escape. Strangely, I'd never thought of Mom as being smart when I was growing up, but now she was showing skills I never knew she possessed. Though she was mentally challenged, she showed a remarkable ability to convince people that black was white. I recall one such time when she got past the hospital guards wearing only a fur coat. Somehow, she managed to make her way to our apartment, where I made her comfortable until the hospital sent over someone to take her back.

For me, the time when I admitted Mother to the hospital was one of the toughest periods in my life. The going was hard and I was alone, except for my friends. My friends - my girlfriends Barb and Maureen and several boyfriends - Erwin, Bob, John, Greg, and Peter - guys I was not intimately involved with but who were there for me all the same - took very good care of me when I moved out of our apartment after Mom's first episode. I learned to count on them, as I never had on my extended family with whom we'd never been close. And slowly, I grew to value my close circle of friends as my family. I couldn't afford another place for a couple of months (a public trustee took possession of our money and mother's property whenever she was in the hospital because I was underage), and during that interim period, I would rotate between friends' homes, where I'd bunk in on a couch and live out of a suitcase.

Naturally, I continued to value my circle of friends as I grew, especially my close women friends, since I made very few female friends in my professional life. That's because after I started my business, I found it much easier working with men - the women I worked with were difficult and sometimes jealous and would try to compete with me in a not-so-honest way. So I slowly became more comfortable in the company of men. Yes, even if men are smoking cigars and swearing and cracking dirty jokes, I find that behavior more real and easier to relate to than being with a group of women who say one thing in front of you and the contrary behind your back.

All my woman friends are special. Of them, Judy, the now late Meredith, Honna and Barbara are a few names that instantly come to my mind, because of the close bonds we share.

Judy, my neighbor when I moved to the suburbs, is an amazing woman with ten children, a number of whom are adopted and of different races. She was a tremendous help when Terri was sick, looking after Jody for hours on end. Back then, our children grew up together. We don't talk so often now, but I will always remember her as being a woman who has a rock-solid faith and belief in God and sees the good in everything.

Meredith was also special - we met through a friend in the late 1980s. She's a perceptive human being who manages to come up with great advice for me whenever we connect, which is fairly often.

Honna and I were introduced in the early 1990s through friends - she's Tyler's sister-in-law now. I only talk to Honna about four times a year, but whenever we chat, she has this uncanny ability to blow me away with her astute observations about me and my life. She makes me sit back and say, 'Wow! How does she know that?'

Barbara in Australia is another special friend who gives me great advice - I have great affection for her.

THIRTY-NINE

To get back to the point that I'm trying to make: though I'm not sure if the mentally ill know that there's something wrong with them, they're aware of what's going on in the world around. And they have feelings too, and an uncanny way of making an impression on people they meet. After Larry proposed to me and I accepted, we needed to introduce his parents to Mom. So I had them over for tea one day when Mother was home from the hospital. Not knowing how she'd behave, I warned them in advance about what not to expect... But they had trouble believing me - Mom played the part of the bride's mother to perfection. She even dug out a silver tea set she'd stowed away someplace.

Larry, of course, got to see her 'other' side. But he was very good with her, even when we no longer saw eye to eye about most things, and he was always ready to sort out the weird goings-on that she got involved with, for which I will always be grateful. One time, mother convinced the manager of the bank holding her savings of $20,000 to allow her to withdraw the money in small denomination bills. Why and how the manager let her do this, God only knows. Anyway, she made off home from the bank with this stash of money that we hadn't a clue about. And after staying at home with us for some time, she accused me of stealing all her money from the bank. I could only roll my eyes. But Larry gallantly stepped in, explained that there had been a mistake, and took off for the bank with all the money packed in a suitcase.

Another time, we received an SOS to hurry back to Toronto when we were on holiday in the States. We rushed over to Mom's apartment on arrival and found two policemen at her front door. I walked in to see white paint flakes everywhere - she had peeled off the coating of all the kitchen appliances with a broom handle. The kitchen cupboards were full of garbage. And mother stood wearing a shower cap and a string of pearls (and otherwise stark naked) in a bathtub as a young, embarrassed police officer stood guard at the bathroom door. Apparently, they'd been standing like that for more than a couple of hours though Mom, of course, had no idea of the time or where she was or what was going on. That's when we decided that she couldn't carry on living the same way.

My feelings for Mother were really mixed up at this time in my life. On the one hand, I'd slipped into the role I'd seen my father play to perfection when he was alive. I protected her, as he had, as best as I could, without complaining, accepting that I had to do what was needed. So, now that I could see that Mother couldn't manage herself and needed ongoing care, we began looking out for an appropriate nursing home - not that that was easy. I was choosy about where we'd put her because my impression of nursing homes is that they are very sad places. Elderly people sit around in halls, some inmates are actually strapped into their chairs, most are on strong medication, and they pass the greater part of the day sleeping. I didn't want that kind of life for her.

On the other hand, I was tired of Mom's games. It seemed to me that she just had to get to know of our being out of town, and she'd pull some antic, and we'd have to ruin our holiday and come back in a hurry. I was tired of making sure that she was all right, of running back and forth between the hospital and her apartment. There were times I thought, 'I'm a young mother, for Pete's sake. Don't you understand how busy I am?'

I had the kids to look after on top of which now I had all this running around to do too - looking up nursing homes and paying extra visits to Mother at the hospital to ensure her wellbeing took up a lot of my time. I felt that I was giving up time that was rightfully Jody's and Julie's, and I resented having to do so. I felt as though I was playing mother to my own mother, which I probably was, and it angered me. It wasn't fair. I was paying back, by mothering Mom, for mothering that I'd never received as a child. These thoughts crossed my mind every now and then, threatening to upset my state of balance.

I thank my sense of righteousness for keeping me going. I couldn't turn away from Mom, I was all she had.

Fortunately, after a long search, I found a nursing home offering decent rooms and staffed by sincere workers. That was Mom's new home and thankfully, she settled in well. The girls were too young to understand her delicate situation, but they'd happily run around Nana when we brought her home a couple of times a year for dinner. And they accompanied me to the nursing home to visit her every Sunday.

All said and done, I spent so much time in mental hospitals and around the mentally ill that I understood how much they need to feel loved, perhaps even more than 'normal' people, to make up for the emptiness in their lives. That's why I was very happy when Mother found a special friend in Bill, a gentleman who ended up in a wheelchair after being hurt in a lumber accident (he fell from a tree). Mom and Bill fell in love, which was very good for them - it brought warmth and a sense of companionship to their lives. Of course, the nurses were always complaining that they couldn't get Bill out of her room, but I turned a deaf ear to these complaints. As far as I was concerned, I was delighted for both. It's never too late to fall in love, as they say.

Mom also experimented with different faiths during the years she lived in the nursing home. Baptist, United, Salvation's Army, and Jehovah's

Witness - it was somewhat amusing to see her change her religion as easily and frequently as changing her clothes. But her actions also helped me realize that she hadn't gone so far on the other side as not to appreciate or feel the need for God.

I wasn't surprised when two days before she passed away from a brain haemorrhage in 1975, a Roman Catholic priest called to ask if I wanted to attend her last rites. Well, of course I wanted to, and wasn't at all fazed that she had converted yet again - Catholicism was to be her last choice. As a result, we ended up having a High Mass with all the bells and whistles to commemorate her passing away. I requested the owner of the nursing home to allow us to hold the ceremony in the recreation room there so that Mother's closest friends from the last decade of her life could attend. It was quite a scene with the residents, most of whom were senile, asking where they were, while my husband's Jewish family was seated in the front row to take communion. If there was one person who was very sad, it was Bill, but even as I comforted him, I expressed my gratitude for the love he had showered on Mom during the years they had been together.

To come back to my visit to that Godforsaken village served by Global Hospital, that's why I felt for the young man locked in the shed, and all the mentally ill people all over the world who deserve understanding and love, not to be hidden away as though they're social outcasts. In the West, most of the homeless people you see wandering on the streets, yes, those very people you brush aside as being nuts, are suffering from some mental illness. They need help.

FORTY

I was pretty adventurous during my second visit to India. I wanted to see more of the country, so after Mount Abu, I made my way down south, where I stayed in a little hotel overlooking the Indian Ocean. It had a balcony hanging over the cliff where I would sit and watch large ships passing by over the course of a day - such a beautiful sight. From there, I traveled across south India from coast to coast, ending my tour in the city of Bangalore, where I was keen to visit a call center servicing the West.

It was fascinating to see about 500 employees occupy small cubicles on the work floor at around 9pm, tune their headsets and start a day's (or should that be night's) work. You know the joke that goes 'If the phone rings during dinner time, it must be a call from India'? It came to my mind as I saw these 500 employees settle down to work that they would probably be making calls to Western nations during the latter half of their night shift. So this was where those dinner time calls we got came from...

I learned that after being recruited, the employees were trained in English spoken with an American accent, which is far from Queen's English but an invaluable skill for these youngsters all the same. Each would end up making about 500 dollars a month, enough for their families to be counted as middle-class Indians.

Another interesting place I went to that makes it to my list of '10 most interesting places to visit in the world' is the north Indian city of Benares or Varanasi. As far as places of historic importance in India go, I'd say that the city is even more enchanting than the Taj Mahal. What gets me is that the beauty of the place comes from the fact that it is chaotic, chaos that works, even if it can leave you (as it did me) with a head swimming in confusion.

The ancient city of Varanasi is the seat of Hinduism, India's most practised religion. Centuries earlier, it was also a major seat of learning. Today, thousands of Hindu devotees visit Varanasi to bathe in the mighty Ganges, the holy river, to cleanse themselves of their sins.

I tried to figure out how this release of sins happens, but it was hard to understand because I saw dead cows floating in the holy waters too, and local residents squatting on the banks doing their laundry and other sundry chores. As a result, words cannot describe the colors of the (dare I say, grimy) waters, but if you have a vivid imagination, you can probably imagine it for yourself. It's a color that contrasts beautifully with the hues of the to-die-for Benarasi silk sarees, spun locally and dried on the rivers' rocky embankment. The point is, how can dirty water wash anything clean, even if the cleansing is a metaphor for repentance?

Another amazing sight in the city is of priests performing the last rites of the dead on the banks of the river. I'm sorry - does this create a rather chaotic picture of the banks of the river Ganges in Varanasi? If so, then I've described it just as it is.

My visit to Varanasi was all the more exciting because I was in the city just days after the Babri mosque was destroyed by Hindu fundamentalists, and the city was engulfed in political riots. The authorities insisted on my being escorted by two armed bodyguards during the two-day visit - that made me feel like a VIP.

These journeys were an eye-opener. Oh, I hated the heat and dust wherever I went - that goes without saying. Also, the bathrooms and the difficulties and discomfort associated with travel. But in spite of all that, I was filled with awe. The posters call it Incredible India. I couldn't agree more. India is a revelation to me because its billion-plus people practising different faiths co-exist in relative harmony, and the country is the world's largest democracy. Not to mention its colors and cultures that are outstanding. You can visit a region, like the south, and feel as though you are in a different land. But north, south, east and west, it's all India. There's another reason why I'm drawn to India - the country has a kind of civility that you don't find in other developing regions of the world, such as Africa. I appreciate that because it's comforting.

FORTY-ONE

I visited Africa for the first time in 1993, a few months after returning from my second trip to India. I traveled to Uganda as a member of a contingent consisting of fourteen Americans, most of whom were from Washington and me, the sole Canadian. We were representing the not-for-profit Food for the World, which had contracted each of us for our skills. Together, we would review Africa's food supply and debt to the USA, and prepare a dossier based on the situation on the ground to brief the former vice-president of the US, Al Gore, as he embarked on his maiden trip to Africa.

Though we'd been informed about the political instability in the country prior to leaving, it was quite another matter to actually be in Kampala and hear about the situation from the horses' mouth, so to speak. People we met told us that things were pretty precarious out in the countryside.

"What about the city?" I asked one of our hosts.

"Cities are relatively safe," he answered.

Nevertheless, I was grateful that we'd been put up at a convent that was tucked away behind tall locked gates. Looking out of the windows of the thick-walled structure at the spiked gates and high walls of the compound, I felt comforted.

Not for long, however. Sometime during our first night in town, I awoke from my stupor to see a small scorpion crawling on the outside of the mosquito netting covering the narrow bed. My instinctive response would have been to scream, only I realized that there was no point - there was no one near enough to hear me and come running to help. We each had separate rooms, and the thick walls of the convent would have prevented my voice from being heard by my nearest colleague. So I gingerly climbed out from under the netting and looked around for a weapon... a broom sitting idly in the corner of the room would do. Somehow, I managed to kill the scorpion (trust me, you don't want to know the details). Then I climbed back into bed.

When our work in Uganda was done, our group went on to Nairobi in Kenya, and from there to South Africa, where we met Nelson Mandela, some of his party leaders, and several senior Government officers.

What hit me the most in South Africa was the blatant corruption - the system that hardly works until palms are greased and even then leaves much to be desired. The poverty also strikes you in the face. You don't have to go looking for it; you simply can't avoid it irrespective of where you travel. To my mind, the people were more downtrodden than in the poorest parts I'd seen of India, and that is saying a lot.

I was keen to understand their social setup, though this wasn't easy because of the racial divisions between Blacks and Whites. Fortunately, I managed to wangle an invitation for Sunday Service at a Baptist Church in a poverty-stricken neighborhood in Cape Town. I was told that I was lucky to see the Church and be a part of the congregation, as it was situated in a barbed-wire demarcated enclosure for Blacks. Whites stayed away from such areas. I was stunned by what I saw. The congregation, garbed in what was so obviously their best dress, or call it their Sunday finery, had an amazing spirit that came through very strongly, in spite of all the hardships they faced. Their enthusiasm lives on in my mind even today.

FORTY-TWO

A few months after returning from Africa, it was time to pack my bags again. I was on my way to India first, as Jahangir had invited me to spend some time with him and his father in his place in Colaba, Mumbai, and then to Nepal and Tibet.

Jahangir lived in an apartment that had large rooms overlooking the city. One room was full of swords he'd collected from around the world. The décor was very Indian with large pieces of furniture (family heirlooms) - it was obvious that he came from a wealthy background.

Jahangir's father was in his ninetieth year. He was a lovely gentleman - I felt so comfortable in his presence. And he told me an ancient legend describing how the Parsi community settled in India many centuries ago. Apparently, when the first Parsi or Zoroastrian immigrants landed in the state of Gujarat in West India and asked the local ruler for shelter, the king sent them a bowl of milk full to the brim, to indicate that his land was already full of inhabitants and could support no more. In response, the Parsi high priest added some sugar to the milk and sent back the sweetened milk. The cup did not overflow, and now, the sugar enriched the taste of the milk.

The high priest had made his point - signaling that the immigrants would adopt local customs and merge with the local people, all the while enriching their lives. I could understand that - I'd felt my own life had been enriched by my soulmate.

But I also felt intimidated by Jahangir's lifestyle, by the four servants and two drivers at his beck and call, and by being looked at from the corner of people's eyes wherever I went. Sure, the servants didn't ask who I was and were very polite, but I'm sure they wondered...

Then my man had to travel to New Delhi for some work and had made reservations for us to stay at the Sheraton (The hotel offered each of its guests personalized stationery - letter pads with the guest's name embossed on it in gold lettering. I thought that was the last word in luxury).

I was under the impression that Jahangir had asked me to accompany him so that we could spend time together after his working day. I had never imagined that I'd get to meet any of his political colleagues. But he had other plans.

One day, we went over to Sonia Gandhi's place for tea. Jahangir introduced me to her as his friend from Canada and actually told her how we had met... she laughed when she heard the story. Sonia was direct in her speech and charming and gracious. She asked about the weather in Canada and why I had traveled to India so often. I felt comfortable chatting with her but wondered what she made of Jahangir's and my friendship...

It was the same story in Kapil Sibal's office, where we stopped for tea the next day. Kapil, a colleague of Jahangir (he's now a cabinet minister), was polite as well, but there too, I wondered what he made of our being together. And the more time I spent with Jahangir, on his home ground, I found myself growing intimidated by Jahangir himself. I wondered what he saw in me when he could have had his pick of any woman, eligible bachelor that he was. I'd ask him that question every so often, and he always gave me the same reply, 'Ah, but you're like a breath of fresh air, my dear.'

FORTY-THREE

I flew to Kathmandu from Mumbai. This leg of my journey was a treat! I celebrated my fiftieth birthday in 1993 and had gifted myself a return ticket to visit Nepal and the roof of the world, as Tibet is called. It may seem a strange birthday gift to give oneself, but then, I'm a woman of eclectic tastes.

I held my birthday party in a small restaurant in Kathmandu with a ceiling so low that I was afraid it would burn down from the sparklers on my cake. Yes, in Kathmandu, people burn sparklers instead of candles on birthday cakes. Adventurous, wouldn't you say?

If at all, it set a precedent for the adventurous trip that followed. I was traveling as a volunteer for Earth Watch, an organization based out of Boston. Our group of six, headed by a crazy anthropologist named Dor, had volunteered to work in four villages on the border of Nepal and Tibet. It was hard weather to be in, freezing cold with only candles to warm up our tents after sunset.

We found the villagers to be very simple folk by virtue of never having interacted with people from Kathmandu, let alone the West. Well-meaning philanthropists sitting far away sent them some useful items like toothbrushes, and some not so useful things like German textbooks. But even the useful items were not appreciated... or should I say, they were appreciated in an unconventional manner. The villagers wore the toothbrushes around their necks as they thought it was some kind of jewelry. And that's kind of sad when you get over the funny part. It just goes to show that you should never take it for granted that people living in different circumstances would understand your way of life. As for the German textbooks, well, I saw some kids supposedly 'read' these. I thought maybe it just made them feel good to look at the books and pretend to be one of us.

We also saw a concrete building that had been constructed with funds made available by the World Bank, but in this project too, the executing team left soon after completing the construction without bothering to earmark the building for a particular use of the community and inform the villagers as such. Consequently, they had no idea what to do with the building, so every day, we were treated to the sight of villagers walking around the building and looking at it with all respect... as though it were some kind of uninhabited temple. But they wouldn't step inside, even on the coldest, windiest and most wintry day when the building would keep them much warmer than they were in their flimsy houses.

One day, the six of us volunteers were chatting about how much more sense it makes for volunteers to personally distribute materials and explain their use when we heard the sound of airplanes droning in the distance. "It looks like more supplies are on their way," I said.

I was right. In the next pass of the airplanes, we saw a parcel being air-dropped. This time, the villagers received royal blue rubber boots. We hadn't a clue as to who had sent the boots or why, we just stood around amused at the sight of kids running around holding boots they reckoned were valuable.

Each of us volunteers had a different role. My job was to try to increase the villagers' awareness of politics by teaching them how to arrange and hold meetings. I did my best; honestly I did and then thought I'd test them by calling a community meeting.

Was the meeting a success?

Yes. The villagers showed up without fail, and only six hours late. All that time, I just cooled my heels on a rock and waited, rolling my eyes every now and then for effect.

All our volunteering was fun but the most memorable event from our week's stay was undoubtedly the cremation of an elderly villager. It's kind of strange to recollect death as an unforgettable experience, especially since it was of a man I barely knew, but you had to be there to appreciate the simplicity and loveliness of the ceremony.

I was really touched when I was asked to lead the funeral procession, which consisted of a long line of villagers walking single file along a river.

We walked for about a mile until we reached a pyre, where the body, covered in white shrouds, sprinkled with perfume and flower petals, was cremated in keeping with Hindu rites.

My visit had been an eye-opener. It helped me understand and taught me to respect other peoples' way of life and culture. And like much of my life, it wasn't devoid of romance. The medicine man the community depended on, he was a Shaman, took a liking to me (if you please). One day, he asked me to meet up with him at midnight (it was a full-moon night) – 'For a reading,' he said.

Well, of course, I was happy to go along with an offer to tell my fortune, and so I agreed... only to scream out loud when later that night, he asked me if I had kids (I replied I had two) and then asked me if I wanted more... talk about being suggestive. I ran a mile before I let up.

All of us volunteers were also very keen to visit Tibet, so we did. But we could only get a Science Visa, which meant that the six of us had to enter the country on foot. It was quite an adventure - a fifteen-mile walk into Tibet, where we met wonderful people who lead such hard lives. We felt privileged to see what we did and so grateful at the same time for the lives we were returning to.

You sure need survival skills to get by in that terrain. People eat far less than the average Westerner when they probably need more calories to keep warm in the cold climate. But they can't afford more. They sleep on the floor of tiny houses made smoky by a complete absence of ventilation (they do that to keep warm). We learned that the average life expectancy in the area was only forty years or so, by and large, because of the hardships the people faced but also because of this singular reason - the smoke got into the villagers' lungs, and they coughed and coughed from an early age. I was taken aback and worked doubly hard to persuade the local World Bank representative to provide the villagers with pipes. Once these were made available, we all worked together to install the pipes in the roofs to ventilate the shacks the people dwelled in.

I remember my journey to Tibet as the time when I learned the value of respecting the earth - it's crucial to the survival of humanity. On my way out of the country, back in Kathmandu, which is one of the most interesting cities in the world in the way it blends the old world and the new, I visited a fortune teller who told me that I would make many trips to that part of the world. He was right. All told, I have visited India twenty-three times since 1990.

FORTY-FOUR

Jahangir and I continued to see each other off and on. In 1994, I recollect we met up in London. Jahangir was there to visit his son, Rehan, who was studying in the UK at the time (that's why I hadn't met him the previous year when I visited Mumbai) and wanted to introduce us to each other. Rehan was tall, just like his Dad, and he was very formal, with a dry sense of humor. And he had a lovely smile that made up for his reserved nature. We all went to St James Palace Hotel for tea and really enjoyed each other's company. I was happy that Rehan was comfortable in my presence.

In my heart, Jahangir was the 'one' man for me, only I knew it wouldn't work because of his and my other ambitions. Sure, we were keeping up our long-distance relationship, but these are really hard to sustain as your life follows no set pattern and you're alone most of the time. That's why Jahangir would insist that I go out with other men. I understood why he said that - he worked like a machine and as a result, as the years went by, we saw less and less of each other.

So it happened that towards the end of 1995, I had a brief relationship with my friend Stan, a drummer who played at nightclubs in Toronto. We'd met and befriended each other two years earlier, but grew closer around this time. I remember Stan as a considerate man, a great cook, an amazing story-teller, and a little full of himself. We were together for a few memorable months.

I remember it was during the months I was with Stan that my friend

Julia's husband Charles died. Julia is a frank and spirited woman I met while volunteering for a campaign. She brought great energy to the election campaigns we worked together on - that's why I felt fortunate to make her acquaintance and her husband Charles is a person who will always stick out in my memory. Julia, Charles, and their five children, all of who were under twelve at the time, lived out in the country in a tiny home that seemed to be falling apart!

Charles was happy to babysit while Julia worked, and it worked out fine for them as he was a great father, a wonderful cook, and an amazing baker who made the most delicious cakes. I really appreciated the way Julia and Charles managed their lives; they didn't have much by way of material possessions but the love and caring between the parents and five children was a pleasure to see and to be a part of, even during short visits. And of course, Charles was a very special human being, perhaps the first person I met who had no ego to speak of as well as astounding strength of character.

To look at, Charles was every inch a teddy bear or a Santa Claus - cuddly, down-to-earth, warm, essentially someone anyone with a heart would instantly take to. I loved Charles for what he was, and especially loved the fact that he didn't care about what other people thought of him. And I loved knowing Julia and Charles as a couple even if I was slightly envious of their relationship - they shared a perfect understanding and were completely in sync with each other's needs. I'd often tell myself, 'That's how a relationship should be.'

That's also why I was filled with sorrow around this time - Charles had developed cancer, and he was only in his late thirties. I couldn't bear to see him go and their relationship end like that - they should have lived happily ever after. But Charles, bless him, left me in awe even during his last days, he showed such strength of character and body even when I knew he was miserable.

I desperately wanted to do something to cheer up his last days, and so, knowing that his dream was to ride a Harley, towards the end, Stan and I arranged for a few members of the local Harley Club to arrive at their house, as a surprise. We were overwhelmed when 50 bikes arrived. Charles was in a state of shock. The bikers were so kind - they gently put Charles and each of his kids in separate sidecars and took them all out for the whole morning, while Julia and I followed in the car. Charles was crying by the time we got home, and so was I, a few minutes later, when he hugged me to express his gratitude. I'll always be grateful to those bikers.

In return (I believe), Charles gave me an artists' imprint of a beaver (that was his nickname). The impression still hangs on my wall - it'll always have a special place in my heart.

The month after, Stan expressed his need to get married and settle down. Instinctively, I knew that it was time for me to move on too. We parted in the best possible way ever - he made me a lovely wooden necklace that said 'I love you. Good luck'. And I promised to always be there for him.

FORTY-FIVE

Another highlight dating back to 1995 was my third visit to Mount Abu. Yes, believe it or not, I spent another fun-filled fortnight with the Brahma Kumaris, hanging out with friends, visiting more villages, and for the first time, learning more about the mystical side of the Brahma Kumaris.

The Brahma Kumaris have complexes at Mount Abu as well as at the foothills at Abu Road. The latter complex houses a special hall, Diamond Hall, which is like a huge airport hangar seating 20,000 people or so. The hall is used for special events, specifically for meetings with a power they say is none other but God (yes, God), eight to ten times a year. At a pre-scheduled time, 20,000 people dressed in white gather in the hall (trust me - it's a sight, a veritable sea of white). A senior lady member of the organization, a colleague of Dadi Janki, called Dadi Gulzar, sits up front on stage. The lights are dimmed, hues of red light filled the hall, and as everyone meditates, Dadi Gulzar goes into a trance, and apparently, God (who they explain to be a supreme energy) takes over her bodily faculties and speaks.

I will never forget the meeting I attended. I had a seat in the front row, and when the sermon was over, I had the fortune of filing past this energy. I tell you, you could see right through Dadi Gulzar as she sat on the stage in a trance. To me, it seemed as though her body was made of light, and I trembled from head to toe when God held my hand (a special privilege). I was filled with a sense of awe. I just couldn't explain what I'd seen neither then nor now that I've attended several similar meetings since.

Dadi Janki, Dadi Gulzar and other founding members of the organization are now in their late 80s and 90s and have been meditating all their lives. I believe they are powerful souls though I acknowledge that seeing is believing. I'd never have believed their strength had it not been for the personal interactions with Dadi Janki that I've had the good fortune to have.

FORTY-SIX

It was a pleasure to be privy to the ins and outs of Jahangir's political career and through him, to the political setup in India. In turn, I hoped to introduce him to the political scene in Canada, which interested me no end, as I thought he would enjoy it.

That's why we ended up spending two days in Ottawa during one of Jahangir's visits to Canada in 1996. We visited the houses of parliament, and I had him introduced from where we were seated in the gallery during a session. The minister of finance did the honors and my man did me proud. Dressed in grey slacks, a navy blue double-breasted blazer, and an ascot around his neck, he really looked the part (and gorgeous). Jahangir was fascinated by the differences in the way politics was gone about in Canada and India.

I also took him to see the War Museum because of his love of history and swords, which he really enjoyed. And as it wasn't all play for me in Ottawa, he had a chance to see how I worked.

I had a client in Baffin Island in Northern Canada - a beautiful place, but so far north that it costs at least $2500 to reach the island from Ottawa. And even then, the amenities are not so tourist-friendly. Just the hotels, for instance, are not of the same standards as in the southern part of the country.

I'd asked Jahangir to accompany me on a trip to see my client. It was one of about four visits I made to the island over the course of a decade, to help implement a health project. I recall that during one visit, I was informed that people were getting killed on the ring road surrounding the town because it hadn't been fitted with lights. That made me sad, and then I wanted to do something about it. So when I next passed through Ottawa, which coincided with the visit I made with Jahangir, I met the minister of transportation and requested him to consider installing lights on that road. Fortunately, he accepted the suggestion.

I'd like to think that my intervention saved a lot of lives. I know that sounds a tad egoistic, but it goes to show that if you genuinely care for people, you'd help if you could. You wouldn't just turn a deaf eye or a blind eye to a pressing issue. After all, they say that great injustices happen when good people stay quiet... I reckon that staying silent when you have the chance to do good is an injustice in itself.

FORTY-SEVEN

The year 1996 stands out in my memory for another reason - it was then that I heard about a fantastic package deal from Air Canada. The airline was offering an around-the-world business class ticket for about $5000. I was smitten by the thought of traveling the world - it sounded so exciting.

I had to do it.

So in June, I embarked on a six weeks round-the-world trip, all by myself.

A journey around the world may not seem like the kind of voyage most people would make alone, but I was happy to go solo. Life has taught me many things after my divorce, one of the most important of which is how to live alone without feeling lonely. There is a popular philosophical saying in India that goes something like, 'We came alone, and we have to go alone.' I like that, as it sort of encapsulates why it makes sense to be comfortable and content with your own company. It doesn't mean that you shouldn't enjoy the company of other people, but the way I see it, it speaks volumes about the fleeting nature of human relationships and why we shouldn't get caught up in them.

My journey started in London from where I flew to Moscow and St Petersburg, then on to Beijing and Shanghai, then Vietnam, Borneo, Hawaii, Los Angeles, and back home.

Here's an honest confession - I was scared some of the time. In spite of that, I enjoyed the adventure, probably because I enjoy the process of learning about people who lead lives that are in stark contrast to mine. I love knowing what makes them tick.

My travels also opened my eyes to a truism that I believe the western world must wake up to, hopefully before it becomes too late, and that is - people in the East consume much less than their counterparts in the West and yet are much happier.

I'm not trying to suggest that consuming less is an infallible recipe to stay happy. I'm just intrigued by the fact that we westerners equate happiness with material success, and we tend to measure success as standing for more. Maybe it's time we started thinking about being happy before being successful, even when we don't possess many 'things'? Anyway, this makes sense to me because if you're happy and love doing what you do for a living, success will sooner or later come your way... If you look at life that way, success isn't the key to happiness. Happiness is the key to success.

And maybe, we could grow more conscious about the resources we consume? (Especially now that economic trends show that we can't be sure of sustaining the momentum we had going before the turn of the century.)

These nuggets of wisdom were the icing on the cake. I'd expected the journey to be a cultural revelation of sorts, and it lived up to that expectation.

I recall sitting in the front row of the opera house in Moscow, on a beautiful seat furnished in blue and gold brocade, seeing Swan Lake being performed. The experience cost me only five dollars (a pittance), but it was priceless in terms of memories.

China, to my eyes, was gray. Life seemed hard, colorless, and bland. The only silver lining was the sight of camels on the Great Wall. That cheered me up no end - I felt as though I was in Disneyland.

The perfumed river flowing through the city of Hui in Vietnam was another precious sight. The Vietnamese are a very gentle people, perhaps that is why I was sickened to no end while going around museums showcasing visuals of ghastly acts that took place during the war - photographs of American soldiers carrying around body parts (heads) of slain woman and children. I found the people very confused about their war experiences. This was before the US re-established its diplomatic presence in the country. I also had the opportunity to climb down to tunnels where soldiers lived for years at a time (I was much skinnier then), and in one city, I stayed in a hotel housed on the third floor of a building that accommodated a brothel on the second floor. Did that bother me? Not one bit, though it was yet another eye-opener.

My memories of Borneo center around a longhouse I stayed in for four days. I actually got to occupy the chief's room (he wasn't in at the time), where I saw a bottle of French shampoo on the counter. Evidently, other overseas tourists had received the same privilege before me! Every day, someone from the longhouse would go fishing to catch my lunch, which was then cooked by elderly bare-breasted women and eaten sitting on the floor in the company of my hosts. Then, it would be time to sit back and watch the evening show.

Yes, my hosts entertained me with a round of drinks (strictly only for the elders). We'd live it up with Johnny Walker scotch. After that, they danced with very long swords, which worried me no end.

Sleeping in the longhouse was especially difficult because of the noise when the shift changed - yup, you read that right. Those who slept at a normal bedtime would be up at three in the morning to go to work while the others who had just come home (at three am) would climb into the very same beds that had just been vacated. They would sleep soundly, undisturbed by the crowing of roosters at dawn, no doubt exhausted after a hard day's work, or should I say hard night's work. But I would lie awake and wonder at their lives.

I consider myself very lucky to have seen all this.

Someone in India once told me that I have four gifts - truth-telling, laughter and joy, inner light, and oneness with life. I think these four aspects blend rather well when strung together, like beads of a rosary. Try it for yourself:

The inner light, which is nothing but life itself, is ever joyous as long as you live in the company of truth. Then, you also find it easy to connect with life as it pervades our world, the quintessential oneness of life.

Essentially, it all starts within.

I cannot thank my travels enough for having steered me in the right direction. Evidently, an extroverted approach worked for me. I started out with an interest in seeing the world. That was my only motivation. But as I traveled, I became more understanding of the situations other people face. It was as though a lot of processing began to happen in my head. Then, from understanding others, I grew more aware of the spark of life that pervades all of humanity and myself, and certainly, I became more giving towards those in need.

Carl Jung once said, 'He who looks outside dreams and he who looks inside awakens.' Dreaming seems to have helped me wake up. But as I still do not consider myself to have awoken fully, I travel on in the hope of maybe achieving enlightenment.

FORTY-EIGHT

Stan did me proud. While I was touring the world, he found himself a wife (it amazes me that some of us find it so easy to get permanently hitched). I was delighted to stand up for him at his wedding on my return from 'the world.'

The month later (it was August 1996, I'll never forget), I received a surprise telephone call from Gerry. I couldn't believe my ears when I heard his voice. We hadn't spoken in ages.

I'm sorry. I haven't introduced Gerry as yet, have I?

Gerry... what can I say about Gerry?

*That my relationship with him has convinced me that we **do** have karmic accounts to settle with certain people who cross our paths?*

That it is amazing how close you can be to a man and still not be able to help him when he is hurting within?

That he is the closest I ever came to marrying again?

I guess the answer is all of the above, and more.

I first met Gerry in December 1986. He was a client I'd been introduced to by Larry Miller, a member of the Home Sewing Association, an industrial group. Gerry was one of the elected members I interacted with when the association approached me to conduct a market study. I must confess that at the outset, I wasn't impressed in the least by his 5'7" slim build and good looks. He would fall asleep at meetings and show scant interest in anything or anyone other than himself. That was it - he was so full of himself and I didn't like that one bit.

But then I had to spend some time alone with him. The association owed me $4000, and so, when Gerry suggested that he'd hand me the cheque over dinner, I could hardly refuse.

We met at a steakhouse. It was a never-ending dinner - we talked and talked. Gerry paid me a lot of attention, which I loved. In retrospect, however, I think that I was so naïve. A worldly woman (something I may have grown to be today) would have sensed that Gerry was putting on the charm just because he wanted to sleep with me. But back then, all I knew was that I was attracted to him, big time. And I wasn't sure if only I felt that way.

It was cold and snowy outside when we finally left the steakhouse - call it the perfect occasion for him to impress me some more. You see, Gerry had a new Jag parked in the lot... only it wouldn't start! So we called the Motor League and I left it at that. I drove home, leaving him to get his car fixed.

We dined again the next week. Only that time, we didn't part ways outside a restaurant on a cold wintry evening. We made it to my house, where we fell into bed and made love for hours.

FORTY-NINE

That started our affair... though for all the wrong reasons. I was taken in by Gerry's charm and by the fact that he drove a racing green Jag convertible, that he indulged me during gourmet dinners and taught me about wine, that he ordered a bottle of champagne when he met my kids for brunch, that he was great in bed, and that he booked the best hotels for us to stay in when we traveled.

I was a different person in 1986. Quite clearly, I valued all the wrong things in those days. That's why I chose the wrong sort of men. Wrong - from my present point of view. But they (Gerry, in this case) were right for the kind of person I was then. I call those days the 'egoistic' period of my life - both my professional and personal life.

I couldn't have had it better on the work front. I'd acquired a few top of the line clients who were happy with my work - that was a major plus, so I thought of expanding my office from a fancy building at Church and Bloor to larger premises in an older building on Isabella. I actually coughed up $200,000 for a third of the office and two lawyers chipped in for the remaining area. I was so enamored of the new premises that I held a fancy party to inaugurate it. And yes, I invited the Who's who of Toronto to celebrate with me... I sure had a big ego back then.

My personal life was no better. I had three men I was simultaneously dating at the party; I agree, that's awful. Gerry was one of those men, Tyler was the second (I was dating him around the time all this happened), and don't even ask me who the third was.

My affair with Gerry was hard on teddy bear Tyler, and he was not the one to take things lying down. He had his own childish ways of dealing with things, and of making it clear that he didn't approve of Gerry. One night, when Gerry was over at my place, Tyler came by and let the air out of all the tires of Gerry's Jag. Gerry never figured out what had happened, but I tell you I had my doubts.

In retrospect, I realize that I should have paid more attention to what Tyler had to say. But I was so caught up in my ego that I turned a deaf ear to anything he (or anyone else) said. I thought that Gerry and I were great together. I felt like my thirst for him would never be satiated - he always left me wanting more. We saw each other a few times every week and talked to each other all the time. He was very charming and I quite thought he was the one, the white knight I was still waiting for, still looking for.

I was foolish, of course. Tyler was right - he wasn't the right sort of guy for me, nor for any other woman. You see, Gerry was married, though you could never have figured that out from the way he behaved.

I was taken aback and felt decidedly uncomfortable when I learned about his marital status. My sense of unease must have been apparent because he then took it upon himself to sweet-talk me into believing his side of the story. Whenever we were together, he'd tell me how unhappy he was, how his marriage had got off to a bad start from day one, how it was all wrong and how our being together was right.

At first, I agreed with him. We seemed to be doing fine as a couple – I enjoyed every minute we spent together. At the same time, I engaged in other facets of my life.

After I bought a larger office, I began thinking of buying a larger home. So it came about that I bought a lovely home in the beach area of the city, in 1987. It was a beautiful place, a three-storied house built in a contemporary style with lots of glass and high ceilings. It was showy, but I didn't have a problem with that. My new home was a great place to host parties. I remember the guest list for my first Christmas party ran to about 100 family members and friends. We'd agreed that each invitee would bring an ornament for my two-storey-high tree. It was very beautiful and special, all the more because I was celebrating Christmas after more than two decades (since I'd converted to Judaism).

This was when I made friends with Anthony (Ant, my India guide) and his wife, Michelle. They were my neighbors and great company. Anthony was the president of an ad agency at the time (he's a little nuts in a good way but has been a special friend all these years).

FIFTY

They say that all good things come to an end... and so it was for Gerry and me (though maybe our being together wasn't such a good thing).

About eight to nine months later, reality began to sink in. I wasn't happy being the 'other' woman in the life of a much-married man. It didn't satisfy my ego. I realized that Gerry might cry foul over his marriage, but he'd been married close to thirty long years for Pete's sake. And he still didn't seem ready to give up his bad marriage, supposedly for the sake of his kids because he shared a close relationship with his son and cared a lot for his daughter... but how would I know? He'd said that he'd brought them up himself and that his wife hadn't contributed much. But I no longer believed him because I'd seen that he was hardly around for his family, he traveled so much.

As it turned out, our affair was probably harder on me than on poor Tyler. But he had me to blame, I had no one. I'd brought my misery on myself, as it happens when you make decisions for the wrong reasons (such as to indulge your physical senses).

My decision to buy the new office turned out to be a disaster too. I'd bought it to show off and celebrate my success. Gerry had thought it was a good investment and had actually helped negotiate the deal as well as invested in the property himself. We both ended up losing money on the property.

When that happened, I decided that I'd had enough of fancy offices and that it would be easier to work from home. I hired an assistant, Judy (who occasionally still works on special projects for me) and Doreen, my book-keeper till now. Operating from home worked out well for me - it didn't bother my clients, who continued to be satisfied with my work. So I ended up reducing my overhead expenses.

By a year later, that would be 1988, Gerry and I had grown very close. I felt drawn to him in every conceivable way, which only made it harder to accept that I couldn't have him for myself. But Gerry was unwilling to reconsider his stance on his marriage... leaving me with no choice but to withdraw. I couldn't stand the idea of living in a state of limbo any longer - it was doing nothing for my free spirit. And so, I finally broke up with Gerry, telling him I couldn't carry on the way we were.

A few weeks after we broke up, life showed me that I'd made the right decision. I was driving down the highway coming home from my friends' cottage in the country when I passed his car parked by the side of the road... he was with a woman. It was a late Sunday morning. I'd heard that his wife was having major back surgery the next day, so I called him and left a message. I couldn't control myself. "You should be at the hospital with your wife, not fooling around," I screamed.

I was still hurting.

FIFTY-ONE

Close to a decade had passed since Gerry and I had broken up. I'd run into him occasionally, usually while in transit in airports, but that defined the extent of our contact.

Now, hearing his voice on the phone, I asked him if he had the wrong number. I'll never forget his reply, he said, "I want whatever relationship you want - friend, lover or partner. I'm leaving my wife."

Well!

I was taken aback, but then on second thought, maybe not. In spite of the lows of our time together, I'd always felt that Gerry and I could have been so good together, if only he'd been willing to formally put an end to his dead marriage.

Gerry wasn't all bad - no person is. What I liked most about him was his quiet strength and his knack of slowing me down and making me think. When I faced difficult business situations, he'd say, 'Slow down. Look at both sides of the story, you'll find a solution.' He was also good at helping me handle difficult people by showing me how to look at things in a different way.

I missed all that.

And now, it seemed that he was willing to do whatever it would take for us to get back together. It seemed as if it was time for 'us' to happen again. When we'd parted ways, I had felt like I was walking away from 'unfinished' personal business, as though we still had some karma to settle.

And now, I could have his positive presence back in my life without being the 'other' woman if, that is, Gerry lived up to his promise of leaving his wife and got his act together as far as his girlfriends were concerned.

Was I willing to take the chance?

I was. So, I agreed, let's just say for old time's sake, to go out for dinner at our favorite waterfront restaurant. We talked and talked over a leisurely meal (so much like our first dinner together), and as we chatted, I realized the inevitable had already happened but for actually happening - Gerry and I were back together, but in what manner and for how long? I wasn't quite sure.

We decided to go away for the weekend and maybe enter a 'same time next year relationship.' So we traveled to Washington DC and enjoyed an idyllic weekend together during which we realized that the 'same time next year' idea would not work.

There had been other men in my life since we parted, Jahangir and Stan. One of these, Jahangir, was still very much a part of my life, and Gerry was seeing other women (on top of which, he was still married).

I couldn't let myself get taken in by his false promises. I couldn't enter into a casual relationship. I knew it wouldn't satisfy either of us. So I gave him my conditions. I told him I was interested in him, but he'd have to clean up his life. I also told him about Jahangir, and I told Jahangir about Gerry. Jahangir was very understanding. He said, "I understand, I'm not there, and you have to do whatever you have to... "

I'd like to think that I was calling the shots now, that is, with Gerry, but even thinking so would be stupid... especially when it was around this time that I was learning that there are some things in life that we have control over and some that we don't. My material needs, for instance, were in my control. And now that I'd realized that I needed much less than what I'd accumulated around me, it was time to scale down. I kick-started the process by deciding to sell my home.

The reason I gave anyone who asked was that the house needed a lot of work, and I figured that I wouldn't get my money back if I sold it after putting more money down on it. I was wrong in that sense - I would have at least doubled my money if I'd held onto the place.

But I was in a learning mode then. Sure, I'd been in learning mode for the greater part of my life, only now, I was learning to see life and my own place in the greater scheme of things in a different light.

So I asked myself, 'What does one person need a large house in the beach area of the city for?'

And the answer I heard was, 'No reason. One person doesn't need such a large place. A small apartment would do fine.'

My big house days and my big party days had come to an end. I shifted to a small apartment in a beautiful heritage building on Balmoral Avenue, in the middle of the city.

A few months later, in 1997, Gerry finally left his wife and moved in with me. I'd agreed to this, of course, but after he actually moved in, I began to have second thoughts. My own experiences had taught me that anyone going through a divorce must first learn to live alone and get together with a new partner only after that. Gerry was still sorting out his divorce, so I thought he needed to go through that period too. Fortunately, a few weeks later, an apartment on the floor below mine became available, and Gerry rented that. We became the upstairs-downstairs couple.

Please understand this - we weren't a perfect couple; we were just chugging along in our own inimitable style. It took Gerry time to clean up his life and I was still seeing Jahangir, though not more than twice a year. I agree, that doesn't say much for my value system. But I was learning. Slowly.

FIFTY-TWO

My India visits and my round-the-world tour had shown me the disparity between the developed and undeveloped worlds. Close to five years had passed since the time I'd fallen sick and been admitted to the Global Hospital in Mount Abu... but even now, I couldn't brush aside images of the poverty I'd seen, and the fact that a little money, if put to good use, can go a long way to alleviate sickness and pain. The hospital's community outreach programmes involving the use of mobile clinics staffed by a doctor, pharmacist, and driver team served many remote rural areas in that part of Rajasthan. Poor village patients would consult the doctor and be prescribed and dispensed essential medication.

The financial aspect of the program is what intrigued me the most. The doctors had told me that the cost of buying medical supplies for a village of about 100 people for a year worked out to about $1000. Now that my business was doing so well, I found myself thinking about this more and more. I could no longer tell myself it was something I'd look into later in life.

I wanted to set up a foundation to collect donations and channel them to people in need. My goal was to help people believe in themselves by giving them a leg up in life. I was keen to reach out to needy people in far-flung corners of the world, not just in North America but in Asia and Africa as well.

It was a noble thought but not so easy to accomplish. Realizing that I couldn't go it alone, I asked every well-placed contact of mine to help. John Birbaum helped develop a concept for the foundation. He advised me to use a painting I had done years ago at Esalen, of a globe surrounded by children holding hands, as the charity's logo.

The going was more difficult in government circles. The government was very suspicious of my proposal since I'd described our concept as being to fund small projects directly, not through other larger (and well-known) charities. To cut a long story short, my friend Jim Peterson, a Federal Member of Parliament and Minister of Finance, was the one who eventually cut the red tape and convinced Revenue Canada that I was not a flake and would be responsible for my donations.

Still, it took all of two long years for us to finally receive our charter. The People Bridge Charitable Foundation came into being in October 1998. But receiving the charter was just the start. I was soon to realize that running a charity is a lot of hard work and a huge responsibility (even though it's well worth the effort).

I formed a Board of Directors with friends from my early work days - Karl, Ken, and Jeffrey - to share some of the responsibility and bring fresh ideas into the working of the charity. At a later stage, Warren, a businessman I'd met through a client who went on to become a business associate of Gerry, also joined the Board. We also formed a group of Honorary Advisors consisting of our friends from four sectors - education, not-for-profit, government, and corporate. Their role was to spread the word of our activities and help raise funds for our projects. Of course, at the outset, I had to set the ball rolling by fund-raising among friends. And I quickly learned that it was much easier to find projects to fund than to raise funds.

I'll never forget our very first project – for the benefit of lepers in India (remember my taxi experience in 1990?). It happened this way:

One day, I received a phone call out of the blue from a lady named Lalita Arya, who'd heard about the foundation from a mutual friend. Lalita was an Indian living in Canada who'd worked with lepers for many years, even though she was almost blind. She was part of an organization called KHEL, short for Kindness Health and Education. She told me that a nutritious, balanced diet could help lepers and so could penicillin. So that became the aim of our first project - to make sure that a village of lepers in Dehradun in India was fed and had adequate medication.

This, and many other People Bridge projects that followed may seem like small endeavors, but that is what the foundation was all about.

Setting up the foundation made me feel good about myself. It made me more responsive to people in need and over time, less indulgent of my own desires. It also made me want to see the world from a different perspective. As a result, my choice of travel destinations changed. After People Bridge was born, I preferred to visit underdeveloped nations to understand the plight of their people and see the conditions on the ground for myself.

Jahangir used to tease me about People Bridge, saying I was helping people for the right reasons, not to get elected to a constituency... He was thinking of politicians in India who put money down on development projects just to get into the good books of their electorate.

Gerry went out of his way to help me get the foundation off the ground - he even paid my part-time assistant's salary for a year. But every now and then, he'd quite frankly say that he didn't understand why I was driven to start the foundation. He'd suggest, 'Why don't you just focus on your business and make money?'

I couldn't, especially not now that my eyes were beginning to open to the oneness of life.

FIFTY-THREE

It was also in the year 1998 that I spent sleepless nights worrying about Julie. One day, I heard that she'd bought an escort service called Sweet Dreams. The very thought made me shudder. 'But no,' I thought to myself, 'It must be some kind of silly prank.'

Julie was given to doing such antics. When she was in school, she once decided that she'd take a taxi to school every day - down five blocks! Jody, even if she knew, didn't tell on Julie, and so it came about that I didn't know what was going on until I got the bill. Needless to say, I put an end to that faster than you can say Jack Robinson.

I hoped that the latest news was also some kind of joke.

But as it turned out, it wasn't.

It was time to have a few words with Julie. I called her over to explain why her choice of 'business' wasn't to my liking. The funny part, if you can call it funny, was Julie telling me in all earnestness, "But mom, the 'ladies' are respectable women. They're all students and young mothers..."

I just closed my eyes and said, "Even so, it's not a smart idea."

The fact that Julie and I share a great rapport - we're more like good friends than mother and daughter - helped me convince her to give it up (though she took her own sweet time to switch 'careers').

But that wasn't all. Julie used to give her father and me much reason to worry back then. We suspected she was into drugs, and she drank too much and went out with all the wrong sorts of men. We were always on tenterhooks hoping the worst wouldn't happen. That's why I was so delighted when Julie got married in 1998. Sure, it was her second wedding... to the same man, George.

Julie and George had first married two years earlier. No, it wasn't a family celebration (else it would've made it to this book a few chapters earlier) because they got married in a city hall for immigration purposes... George paid Julie $5000 for his change in status...

Funnily enough, they started seeing each other soon after, and now we had a reconfirming wedding with all the trimmings. My good friend and Anglican priest Prue married them in what was a lovely ceremony. George had a stabilizing effect on Julie's life and an overall positive influence on her. He was a hard-working guy - he held two jobs. In my opinion, he's a gem, and she was lucky to have him.

FIFTY-FOUR

Jody, unlike Julie, was doing very well. She studied marketing and after working for a few years, launched her own business from scratch. She never looked back.

Jody invested wisely in her company and her personal property, acquiring a warehouse, office building, and a million-dollar home (I fondly call her my mini tycoon). And she hopped on to the 'do good' bandwagon before me, though for different reasons. Jody saw that businesses that engaged in charity could build a stronger brand name and so began supporting charities working for the homeless a few years before I launched People Bridge.

But more than that, I'm happy that strong-willed Jody has never let her business successes, awards and whatnot stand in the way of her family life. She manages to hold it all together, which, to my eyes, is a great achievement.

Jody, with her first husband, Lorne, who she married in 1992, share two wonderful children, Spencer and Dawson.

Jody had a full-time baby nurse when Spencer was born, and as she went back to work soon after, she employed a nanny for the baby too. Gerry and I would go over at least once a week to do whatever we could - to hold the baby, walk the baby, and so on. I loved that.

I love being a grandmother. It's a wonderful feeling, in many ways, better than becoming a mother. You have no pressure and can just enjoy watching your grandchildren grow. And being a grandmother gives you a chance to make up for any deficiencies with your grandchildren. Since I never rated myself as having been a great mom, I welcomed the opportunity to make up for my past mistakes.

FIFTY-FIVE

Jahangir visited Canada again in September 1999. We saw each other less and less because he was working so hard, about eighteen to twenty hours a day, and found it hard to take out time to travel overseas. I worried about him but accepted that there was nothing that I could do to help him. That's why I was delighted to spend time with him and for him to have the opportunity to relax. I told him how close Gerry and I had grown, and he was so sweet, he kissed my cheek and said, "My dear, I just want you to be happy."

I was never to see him again. Early one morning, about three weeks later, I received a fax from his secretary saying that Jahangir had died of a heart attack.

His last rites would be performed in keeping with Parsi tradition. I couldn't bring myself to fly to India to be present for that - the very thought of his body being put on the parapet of a wall to be picked clean by vultures sickened me. I couldn't bear to see that kind of an end for a man I had loved so much. So I just sent a condolence message to his son, who'd grown to be a fine boy.

Gerry was a huge support at this difficult time of my life. I felt grateful to have him by my side.

FIFTY-SIX

My white knight Gerry was also supportive of my work and took a keen interest in my travels. It's true that he didn't join me on my overseas sojourns, but then his business took up a lot of his time. I'm also not sure how comfortable he would have been - traveling in underdeveloped regions is not always easy, and frankly, I'd only want a companion who was comfortable with the going. In fact, sometimes, it can be downright scary. Like once when I was on my way out of Kenya, I stepped out of the hotel with my baggage and sat down in the car that had been arranged to take me to the airport. I'd just about settled in the back seat when a young guy put a gun to my head through the window of the car. He wanted to rob me.

I was terrified - what made it worse was that the driver of the car had gone off for a few moments, leaving me alone. Then by a stroke of luck, this burly bodyguard standing at the entrance of the hotel, which was hosting a contingent of Sudanese politicians taking part in a conference, saw what was going on and strode over to where we were, picked the guy up by the scruff of his neck and literally threw him on the ground. I watched the proceedings with my eyes wide open, shaking from head to toe. Gosh, how badly I wanted to get home!

My flight back was to New York. Gerry and I had arranged to meet up there - little had I known when we planned it that way that I'd be a complete mess when I reached. Anyway, Gerry took one look at me and said, "We're going to a movie." I thought he was nuts, there was no way I'd manage to sit through a movie in that frame of mind. But strangely enough, it was the best thing to do. We went to see a Jim Carrey comedy and I laughed for two straight hours - talk about getting things out of the system, the movie turned out to be the best therapy!

But to come back to my story, that's why I always left the choice of coming or staying back to Gerry, without putting any pressure on him at all. More often than not, he opted out. That's why I traveled alone to Bali and Australia in 2000.

Bali was special. I saw this painting there - a 5 feet by 5 feet painting of an Indian temple at dusk, showing the holy premises beautifully lit up for the evening prayers with a few shadowed corners for contrast, and people hurrying to enter it - and thought, 'I must have that for my collection.'

My art collection is very important to me. Decades ago, when I was 19, I took an art appreciation course which helped me realize that art is such an isolating process - artists work on images they see in their heads. It's entirely up to them to choose the brush strokes they need to bring their visions to life. Art starts within and is first executed within, at every step of the way. It's not easy for artists to achieve something they're comfortable with and proud of, kind of like writing this book...

A gentleman I once met in Europe spoke of himself as being an artist of life - I love that term because it suggests that our lives are entirely in our hands, a work of art we are solely responsible for.

Coming back to my art collection, I only seriously began collecting art after my divorce, possibly because I had control over my finances only after separating from Larry. I also kept far busier when I was married. I came across one of my first pieces of art in 1987, soon after I'd bought the house in the beach area.

I was approached by a seller of a painting titled 'We are all one' by a Canadian Inuit artist. The title is as appealing to me now as it was then - isn't it lovely? It's an adage I believe in from the bottom of my heart. Only, the price was lovely too - at $4000, the piece was way too expensive for me, but I somehow managed to buy it. Today, the same work is worth about $35000, not that its revised price tag has inspired me to sell it. It still hangs proudly on my wall amid over 70 works by artists from across the globe, picked up during my travels. Over the years, I've learned that you don't necessarily need piles of money to collect art and it's important to trust your instinct, which means, buy what you like.

So I bought the temple painting in Bali, and packed it with care and sent it home - I recall the shipping cost me more than the art. Today, the piece hangs in the foyer of my apartment. I sometimes think that I'd like to bequeath a piece of art for each of my friends to have when I die.

BETTY STEINHAUER

FIFTY-SEVEN

From Bali, I traveled to Port Moresby, Papua New Guinea, to explore a potential People Bridge project - to provide crutches to disabled children. That leg of my journey went off very well. Then, it was time for some sight-seeing. I'd planned to tour a jungle. But it was not to be...

I reached the point from where we were to leave for the jungle and spent almost an entire day with the tour operator (which bored me to death). Every time I asked, the guy was quick to reassure me that the other members of the group were on their way. So I waited, and waited...

But when no one showed up by late afternoon, I began to feel jittery. I decided that I needed to leave, then and there. Armed men, members of local militia gangs that virtually ruled the place (pretty much a la Wild West, wouldn't you say?) were milling around all over the place. That only accentuated my fear. So I headed straight for the airport, which was jam-packed, where I was told that all of the next few flights out to Australia were fully booked.

What next?

Oh, I found a way out. I slipped the airport manager a one hundred US dollar bill, and he smiled. Ticket in hand, I smiled as well. (Please don't miss the moral of this story - always keep a few hundred dollar bills handy when you're traveling in foreign lands because you never know...)

In Australia, I made my way to a mountainous region in the north, near Darwin. I was keen to climb those mountains to see some Aboriginal art painted on the walls of caves tucked between the peaks.

I met a special and unusual lady named Claire on this trip. Unusual because when I first met her, she was chanting to the mummies in the rocks. I smiled to see what she was doing... Evidently, she had her own inspiration for making this journey.

Claire was sweet and we became good friends during the one week we traveled and lived together in the bush (we are still good friends). It's a pity that I can't say the same for the flies.

All in all, my sojourn in the bush was a life-changing trip. I learned a lot about the Aborigines' love for the earth and their way of life - it's so tolerant and adjusting. I saw an entire community of Aborigines, around fifty people, live peacefully together in a not-so-large house... and to think that we find it hard to live together in twos and threes. I'm not sure if the word 'spoilt' even begins to describe us.

The views from the top of the mountains were spectacular, and for some strange reason, brought back memories of Jahangir. Not quite a year had passed since his death, yet in all those months, I'd never openly mourned his passing away. Now I understood why. The setting hadn't been right. In my busy life in Toronto, I'd never felt the need to come to terms with his passing away. And even if I had, I doubt that I would have been able to get it out of my system, because my mind would have been caught up with so many other things that it wouldn't have been able to focus. I had just felt sorrow and not 'treated' the sorrow, so to speak.

Sitting amid nature up in those mountains, I sobbed for about half an hour as I finally bid adieu to Jahangir, my soulmate. An amazing man I'd truly loved and respected.

FIFTY-EIGHT

A few months later, I traveled to Africa for the second time in my life to check on the progress of a few People Bridge projects. We'd been approached by several charities for help - now we had a website so people could find us on the internet. Some international divisions of churches also knew about us, and the Coady Institute helped spread the word about our activities too.

We'd already funded supplies of food, housing materials, and medical supplies in Uganda to help rehabilitate flood victims. We'd also met the costs of clothes and sanitary napkins to keep 400 kids (especially girls) in school.

I wanted to see whether the beneficiaries were happy with our involvement and explore a few more potential projects. I was open to new ideas, though I had a vague notion about doing something for people afflicted with HIV. Those were the days when the western media was abuzz with news that HIV and AIDS were spreading like wildfire in African communities, and suggestively put this down to their promiscuous behavior. But naturally, this caused more than a few eyebrows to be raised. I wanted to know whether this was true, and if so, whether the people were really as they were being made out to be or if some other reason was to blame for the sorry state of affairs. My interest grew all the more after I reached Kampala because the young women I saw on the streets when we drove around didn't seem to be 'that' sort at all.

A pastor I met, Fos Dickson, enlightened me about the ghastly circumstances that had led many young women to contract HIV and/or AIDS.

He started out saying, "They weren't born and brought up in the city, you know. They migrated here from their villages in search of employment and safety."

I could understand what he said about wanting to make it good in the city - it was the part about safety that got my attention.

I remembered what a host had told me when I'd visited Kampala seven years earlier, as part of a group engaged by Food for the World - that the countryside wasn't safe. I hadn't gotten into specifics at the time, but now I wanted to understand the situation better.

"Why aren't they safe in their villages?" I asked.

What I learned was that women and especially young girls living in villages dotting the countryside bore the worst of the brunt of rebels roaming the land, plundering, and looting at will. Many of these women and young girls had no male support, husbands and fathers desperate to find work left their families in the country and migrated to cities. When night fell, the elderly, the infirm, the women and the children would huddle to sleep in their shacks, hoping against hope for a night of calm. But there was seldom a night when some village or other was not attacked. The rebels would arrive, in groups of a dozen or more, take whatever they wanted and corner young women of their choice. These girls, some as young as 12, were raped, over and over again, and sometimes, during successive nights.

That explained the sullen cowering look on the faces of a few young women Fos introduced me to. They had all run away to the city after being raped, fearing for their lives. Some of them had already lost their parents to AIDS and had lived with elder sisters or members of their extended family until they fled. Now, they feared death the same way as their parents. Their self-esteem was as low as you'd expect it to be, given their ordeal, and they were so obviously not interested in themselves or in dating, as you'd expect a young woman to be. Fos said that they'd been scarred for life.

It was depressing, and somehow, so ironic. The men who left their families in the country to seek employment in cities often contracted HIV from having sex with prostitutes. Back home, bereft of the support of their men, women failed to protect their young daughters, and sometimes themselves too, from the wrath of the rebels. Many of them contracted HIV from being raped, again and again. I felt very disturbed to hear all this and could hardly sleep that night. I lay awake in my bed for what seemed like an eternity, now entering and then coming out of a state of trance.

As a result, when my alarm went off in the morning, all I could think of was having a sleep-in. But then a sliver of mauve, or was it pink, peeping in from the window caught my eye, and I couldn't help myself from jumping out of bed - it was the sky. I rushed to the window, only to see one of the most beautiful sunrises I have ever seen. As I stood there staring in disbelief, there came to my ears the sound of melodious voices singing in chorus. Shanty dwellers, all migrants from villages, were singing as they went about their morning chores, just as they would have back in their native surroundings. Their tune was simple and devoid of drum beats, but it echoed harmony in every note. In the peace and calm of that moment, I found it difficult to imagine what the morning after must have felt like in villages plundered during the night by rebels. How hard they must have found it to sing. And even if the elders mustered up the courage to face another day, and sought to tell their young ones that life moves on, would their song fall on deaf ears?

I was safe - there was no doubt about that in my mind, the unrest in the countryside had not affected the city. Then why was I feeling so vulnerable?

FIFTY-NINE

Over the next few days, I finalized the details of a project to teach 100 students life skills and fund a water tank for an orphanage. Then it was time to fly to Nairobi in Kenya to meet Dorothy, a lady running Wofak (short for Women Fighting AIDS in Kenya).

Dorothy had first connected with me by email. She'd asked People Bridge for assistance to run Wofak. Her proposal was sound and we'd already funded some Wofak activities. Now I was keen to see the situation on the ground myself, especially as Dorothy had indicated that Kenya was struggling the same way Uganda was, to counter the spread of AIDS and HIV.

Dorothy introduced me to an elderly grandmother struggling to fend for two of her grandchildren after her daughter and two more (younger) grandchildren died of AIDS during the course of a week. This was 'normal,' said Dorothy, seeing my horror-struck face. "Countless families in the area have suffered the same fate."

I felt terribly distraught but desperately wanted to help the grandmother get by and so arranged for People Bridge to bear the family's living expenses for a year as well as the cost for the children to receive some vocational training.

Dorothy was also helping some young girls who had made their way to the city after having been successively raped in their villages. She showed me the large room she had arranged for about 10 such girls. There were 10 mattresses on the floor. A few clothes were neatly folded and kept with personal belongings besides each mattress. The room was clean, if bare. A ray of sunshine playfully danced between two mattresses –it was the only bright spot in the space. Dorothy pointed out a bathroom situated down the hall.

"It's luxury for them," she said. "And they know they can sleep safely at night."

I wanted to meet the girls. Since it was Sunday, a few were hanging around, doing nothing in particular. Dorothy introduced me to them. We didn't talk much, though. The girls would look up at me and then look away as though uncomfortable to meet my eyes. I didn't want to upset them, so I didn't push our stunted conversation further. I gave each girl some pocket money and left more money to buy them food for the next month. Even after doing that much, I returned to our quarters feeling out of sorts.

I tossed and turned in bed before finally dropping off to sleep at what must have been an unearthly hour. And all I could think of when I woke up was to go back and meet Dorothy's protégés again. It was Monday, so most of them were out, working or looking for work, I was told, by a tall, slim girl with short dark hair who was hanging out clothes to dry in the yard. I walked up to her, smiled, and asked, "What's your name?"

"April"

Later, I found out that April wasn't her real name. She was too scared to tell me that.

"Do you like life in the city, April?"

She looked at me and said nothing. Then she shrugged her shoulders, as though to say, "Dunno."

I swear I didn't want to upset her, but something inside me was driving me to talk to April about her circumstances. I found myself saying -

"Don't think about what happened. It's over now. You've got your whole life ahead of you."

In response, April sat down on her haunches, buried her head in her arms, and began sobbing. Then she shook her head from side to side, saying, "It was my fault. I'm a bad girl." She said those words again and again.

I couldn't bear it any longer. Tears welling up in my own eyes, I sat next to her, put my arm around her and held her to me for what seemed like a long time. Then I looked her in the eye and said, "I know what you're going through, April. Trust me, I know. I was raped too, when I was thirteen."

SIXTY

I couldn't believe that I was actually talking about the incident that cut short my childhood and threw me into the big bad world of adults headlong, without any warning.

It was the only blot on what was otherwise a fairly happy childhood.

But my words had hit home. I now had April's attention. She stared at me in disbelief, her beautiful big eyes wide open, as I spoke -

"It happened one Saturday evening when I was thirteen. I was walking to my best friend Barb's home to spend the night and chose to cut through a parking lot to get there quick. That's where it happened."

I paused, not for effect, but because waves of emotion swept over me as I found myself crying, and it was now April who falteringly slung her slim arm around me, not sure if she was doing the right thing but doing so all the same.

Closing my eyes, I continued, remembering every sordid detail of what had happened next and trying hard not to relive the hurt of being abused.

"There were three boys, and no one else was around. I knew two of the boys as seniors at school, and the third was younger to me. They got hold of me and dragged me to a lonely spot in a park where they pulled down my pants and pulled up my top. Then one guy put his penis inside me, another stuffed his penis between my breasts, and I think the third used his fingers. All the while, I felt a rock piercing my back - it hurt, but I preferred concentrating on that pain, not the hurt they were inflicting on me... "

By now, April and I were both sobbing, both in the recollection of our moment of shame. The present and the past seemed to have merged at that moment.

April's gentle piercing eyes looked at me with understanding. She didn't say anything. But I could feel the sense of calm that was dawning on her, as my story showed her that we shared a special bond, a moment of loss that she would otherwise never have imagined I had experienced, and so, I went on.

"They ran away, leaving me bleeding and crying. I was unimaginably hurt and just about managed to walk to Barb's house, where I shared my story with her and then sat in her bathtub for a long, long time. Her parents were out and I made her promise that she wouldn't tell anyone. Ever."

Again, I paused, remembering how confused I had been in the moments that followed. April must have thought that my story had come to an end, but she evidently wanted to know more, for she said, "Then what happened?" And I could sense that she wanted to know how I had plucked up the courage to face the next day.

"I was confused and had no idea what to do. I was scared to tell my parents because I knew my father would have gone after those boys, and God only knows what would have happened then. I ended up telling no one."

"And the boys, did you ever meet them again?" asked April.

"Sure, two were from my school. They made up a tall story about me having led them on, which they narrated with much bravado to any of the kids who'd listen to them. But I was so desperate to protect my reputation that I decided to ignore the boys and act as if nothing had happened. I couldn't bear the idea of the kids believing their tale, and I figured that would serve them right, possibly even take them down a peg or two. That's what happened - no one believed the boys. I was a popular girl and kids thought that the boys were pulling a fast one on them."

Sitting there next to April, I smiled in remembrance of how relieved I had been to have pulled off the act.

"That's why you've got to get on with your life, dear, and I'm glad I'm here to help you do so." I smiled at her, and April gave me a small smile in return.

That evening, I told Dorothy that People Bridge would meet April and a few other girls' living costs for two years, and also the cost of teaching them basic beauty skills, such as doing hair, manicures, and stuff. The smile on April's face when she heard about this was the best thank you I could have received. She'd been through much more than I had, and I desperately wanted her to come through fine. Just knowing that I'd helped start the process of her recovery left me feeling as though a weight had been lifted from my shoulders (Two years later, April was a sought after manicurist in her community and gave me an excellent manicure when I revisited Nairobi. More significantly, she was a changed person - no longer sullen, she was laughing and enjoying life.).

SIXTY-ONE

As I lay down to sleep that night, I thought about the process of moving on and the energy it takes to cope with distress. A few years after I'd been raped, I'd volunteered at a Rape Crisis Centre where we were taught to help women who'd been physically abused. The experience opened my eyes to the sheer number of women who are molested or raped and taught me to reach out to women needing help. So, about a year later, when a friend of mine was raped when a bunch of us visited Nassau, the rest of our group stared at her dumbfounded when we found out about her ordeal. But because I knew what it felt like, she felt free to share the sordid details with me and cry in my presence, which for most, is the first step of the process of getting the trauma out of the system. Now, I'd met young girls who had suffered serial rape, halfway across the world, which just showed how similar situations are created in different countries and peoples.

I hoped April would move on, sooner rather than later. I thought she would because I'd seen that she had the strength of character, which gets you halfway there. Knowing when to use your head helps too. Like when

I was raped, I survived the next day at school because I used my head. If I'd let my heart take over at that point, I would have crumbled. And as for all the emotions and pain bottled up inside, I would never have let it go if I made it a point to always think with my head. There are times when you just have to indulge your heart to be able to let go, and I hoped that April and the other girls would do so, as I had done two years after my moment of shame.

I'll always thank my good friend John for helping me overcome the trauma of being raped. John was a super cool guy and stood out from my friends because he had a mature, kind and gentle persona. He understood what I had been through, and I felt very comfortable in his presence. That's why my stricken self accepted him as the catharsis I needed to overcome the trauma of being raped. Our friendship led to our spending every Sunday afternoon together at his place, wherein his parents' absence, we gently taught each other about sex. And that's when I finally let go of the protective shield I'd put up around myself after being raped, and was able to accept the idea of dating guys. John and I were never really seen among our group of friends as a couple - for some reason, that didn't matter to me. Our togetherness had done a lot for me as it is. Some things in life are never more than what they are - that's why it's not a good idea to read more into them. This was one of those things.

SIXTY-TWO

By the end of the year 2000, it became apparent that Gerry and I were both ready to take our relationship to the next level. For me, I think my travel to Australia enabled me to finally put an end to the Jahangir chapter in my life, which left me feeling lighter. Otherwise, as long as he was alive, even though I was seeing other men, I could never disregard the fact that he - Jahangir - was the one I would have wanted to be with.

I had to face reality. Jahangir was no more. Life had introduced me to my soulmate, I was happy about that. But our togetherness had not ended as fairy tales do, with us living happily together forever after. My soulmate had moved on.

Then I accepted reality - Gerry was by my side. He was my future, and for all his faults, we had a great relationship. Gerry had paid a heavy price for his divorce, but in spite of that, he was very generous towards me. And we were very much in love. So we had a commitment ceremony in late December 2000 in Key Largo, Florida, after which we moved in together.

We were great as a couple. I know I've said this before, but we really were. I would often think of us growing old together, and the thought left me with a warm sense of satisfaction. It helped no end that Gerry got along fairly well with my girls, Jody and Julie, and my grandchild Spencer (and Dawson too after he came along in 2003), and I enjoyed the company of his son David and his family. Gerry and I would have our families over for festivals - these occasions were as much a treat for the children as for us.

Gerry and I looked for opportunities to do things together and travel and have fun, since our working lives were quite hectic and I also traveled alone so much. In 2002, when I bought a house in Newfoundland, a two-storey 120-year old cheery bright yellow, white, and navy blue property overlooking the ocean, Gerry helped renovate the place.

We took to visiting Newfoundland every summer because I loved spending time on the water or interacting with newly acquired friends or just relaxing in the study, even when I visited alone. Newfoundland is very large - it takes a week to traverse the island. But it's a place of immense beauty - I've never seen a similar spot. And its natives are the independent sort, different from Canadians of the mainland (though somewhat similar to the down-to-earth folk who live in Whitehorse, a beautiful place in the northern part of Canada, people who will have nothing to do with visitors who do not respect their lifestyle). The music, art, and culture of Newfoundlanders are different from what you see and hear in Canada's main cities too. It took the local community two years to accept me - until then, they looked upon me as a mainlander.

2003 was also very special because I turned sixty. I remember Gerry took me to a fancy resort on a private island in the Florida Keys, where we celebrated my birthday with a lovely sit-down dinner on the beach served by white-gloved waiters. Afterward, I traveled on alone to Vancouver, Los Angeles, San Francisco, and Australia to catch up with old friends and tour some and in general, indulge myself before I got back to more work for my business and the foundation.

SIXTY-THREE

People Bridge was always under pressure to fund more Canadian projects. Not that we were prejudiced against home projects, but we were able to do so much more with the money we raised in less developed countries. That's why I preferred funding overseas endeavors. But I'd always go out of my way to lend a hand to projects that were close to my heart. Such as when I heard about a program for school drop-outs in Edmonton in 2003. I immediately connected with the authorities for more information to decide if we could help in any way.

I could never hear about school drop-outs, of any race or color, and not remember the time when I was forced to drop out of school at the age of fifteen. It so happened because Dad came home one day with pain in his arms and before we knew what was happening, he collapsed. It was his first and last heart attack at the age of forty-three. The thought that he'd never suffered a sick day in his life made it all the more hard to digest the fact that he was no more.

The ensuing days were some of the hardest periods of my life. I couldn't believe that my father, my friend, and guide had gone, leaving me all alone. He was the one man I admired most for his strength, and now he was no more. You bet I felt alone, more so because Mom had sort of collapsed too. She was lost. In true style, bless her.

Dad's death was a blow I was given no time to recover from because there were so many things to sort out. First, I had his funeral to think of.

Dad had no insurance, so I paid my first visit to the bank to borrow $1500 to pay for putting him six feet under. I spent the hours before the funeral making sandwiches and dessert for the guests who would return home with us. Not to mourn, but to socialize. Seeing people laugh and smile and make polite conversation only made things worse. I just wanted to scream, 'Don't you know that my father has just died?!' I needed to vent, but it seemed so inappropriate amid guests. I hated society for its shallowness. And at that point in time, I hated my life.

I also had no relative to offer me support. My mother dug out a telephone number, her sister's, and asked me to invite my aunt. It was the first time I'd heard of my aunt's existence, and if I thought I'd receive any sympathy from her, I couldn't have been more wrong. Oh, she turned up for the funeral alright. But she was quite a character, with her large floppy hat and skirt and lots of bright red lipstick. She seemed to be playing the part of a hussy, and soon enough, she got cozy with our TV repairman and they left together. I never saw her again.

My emotions stayed bottled up inside. I know it sounds like I was getting on with things alright, managing the situation, as they say. The truth is that I was living in a fog - I just did what needed to be done at the moment. It was all doing, and no feeling, if you get what I mean.

Since Mom had never worked, and it became evident that she was incapable of getting a job, our money worries, and the task of running the household fell on me. I quit school. My teachers didn't like that, but they saw my point and couldn't really argue.

To be honest, leaving school didn't bother me so much. Schoolwork had bored me and I'd never been any good at mathematics or science. In hindsight, I realize that I may have been dyslexic, but I wouldn't know for sure. There wasn't much awareness about dyslexia in those days.

What was tough was the thought of going it alone, of having to take on so much responsibility, and of having lost the single most important presence in my life. Dad had been the center of my world. He'd tried so hard to make up for the lack of hands-on mothering by always being there for me, my rock of Gibraltar offering me steady, solid support. He'd join in, his ruddy complexion standing out and blond locks flying when I played soccer with friends. He'd take us for ice-cream on Sundays. Every summer holidays, he'd pack us into his old car and drive to the country. We stayed at motels, went swimming in lakes, played on the beach and ate a lot of ice-cream. And even though we were working-class people without a lot of money to spare, he went out of his way to fulfil my every request - buying me a little white fur (not real) coat with matching hat and muffler, lots of books, comics, and we were one of the first families in our neighborhood to have a TV. I still remember running home when I saw the aerial on the roof.

Dad was also quite the disciplinary force in my life. He didn't always give in to my demands - I recollect one of my first boyfriends had an ancient car resembling a hearse. When this boy came to pick me up for a date, dad refused to let me go, saying, "The back seat is way too large." That was so cute.

And now he was gone. I'd give anything for one last conversation, and another, and another... but no. Life doesn't work that way.

I had to face the fact that I was all alone and needed to find a job. How on earth would I ever manage that? It seemed a tall order, given that I was only 15 and hadn't even finished school.

SIXTY-FOUR

Thinking that I could make up for my young years by presenting a serious persona, I paid a visit to the head office of Power Supermarkets in the funeral outfit I'd worn for dad's last rites - black skirt, black sweater, lace collar, black pumps. Hopefully, I looked somber enough to show them I was serious about working for them.

Never one to mince words, I told the lady sitting at the front desk that my dad had just died, and I needed a job. She just stared back at me. And then I saw Leon Weinstein, the president of Power Supermarkets walking down the hall helping his aged father balance a bowl of soup. Mr. Weinstein was an imposing figure if there ever was one. He was about six feet tall, very heavy-set with a receding hairline, and a big cigar hanging out of his mouth.

Of course, at that point, I had no idea who this gentleman was. I just thought he looked authoritative, the kind of guy who makes decisions, so I went and stood in his way before the receptionist could shoo me off.

Mr. Weinstein politely asked me what I wanted, so I repeated the line I'd rehearsed in my mind the night before, "My dad has just died, and I need a job to look after my mother."

He looked me up and down and said, "Come with me," in his trademark gruff voice. And that was it... he didn't ask about my education nor about my work experience.

I was appointed office assistant in the office of Leon Weinstein, president of Power Supermarkets, and loved what I did from the word go. I met loads of new people and learned a lot of new stuff. And my employers showed great kindness toward me - Mr. Weinstein's staff also invited my mother to our office Christmas party, not that she attended, but the gesture was very kind.

Soon, I learned to see through Mr. Weinstein's gruff demeanor and stern looks for what he was - a pussycat through and through. Many years later, I mustered up the courage to ask him why he'd given me the job. His reply was that in all of his years in business, he had never had anyone do what I'd done.

Mr. Weinstein's kindness helped push me into a comfort zone. For the first time since Dad died, I felt secure. And I would have been happy continuing that way for a long, long time. But it was not to be, though I mean that in a positive sense.

One year later, Mr. Weinstein told me that I was too bright to continue as an office assistant and encouraged me to find other work. I'll always be grateful for that push even though at the time, I felt a bit nervous. I wanted my next job to be as satisfying as my first and leave me feeling as secure.

I applied for a job with Bell, the telephone company, as a long-distance operator, and was lucky to get selected after the first round of interviews. My stint with Bell was a success too. I rapidly progressed to the rank of supervisor and continued with the company for a few years. (Looking back, I wonder if my fascination and dependence on phones grew out of the time I worked for Bell. At the peak of my career, my friends used to joke about me being buried with my phones when I die - they got so used to seeing me carry around a few handsets no matter where I traveled.)

When I was 18, I was hired as a personal assistant to the president of a large life assurance company. My job was to welcome his guests and supervise the flow of work in his office. It was a great learning experience, for it enhanced my understanding of managing systems. I was working for this company when I met Larry and continued working there until I got pregnant with Jody.

SIXTY-FIVE

The three years from when I was fifteen to eighteen were tough on me, really tough, but in hindsight, left me with the thought that well-meaning parents who try to give their kids a near-perfect 'no tears' childhood could do well to take a breather. The point is that your good intentions may fall short someday because life has a way of springing nasty surprises. That's why I'd go so far as to say that such parents fail even when they succeed in sheltering their kids from pain and sorrow. Like country singer Lynn Anderson suggested, life isn't a rose garden; along with the sunshine, there's got to be a little rain sometime... and that's why I believe a few letdowns during childhood prove useful in the long run. My teenage lows taught me to make life work, even when the going seems out of kilter. Put together, the sunshine and the rain gave me a sound rooting for life as an adult.

And it's not as though you can't make up for lost ground. Around the time I was working for Bell, I decided to make up for having dropped out of school, thinking, 'So what if I have to work during the day? I can make up for it at night.' I was keen to take courses in basic psychology and sociology, so I enrolled myself in a night school. It was a noble idea but it didn't come off that well. I used to drive our professor nuts with all of the questions I asked, such as the meaning of life and all that. Finally, he put an end to my questions, saying that the course was about basic sociology and my questions went too far.

I may not have caught up with my business school graduate peers then, but it didn't matter. I managed alright, learning from whatever I did. The way my life turned out has led me to firmly believe that my having to drop out of school made no difference in the long run. I remember at one point during a meeting with about ten directors of education from across the country, one guy asked me where I'd got my masters degree from. That made me laugh, and I went on to narrate my story - you should have seen the look on their faces! Having said that, I've also always felt my father's presence in my life, protecting me as my guardian angel. After Dad died, his memories stayed with me as energy propelling me forward, egging me on to make something good out of my life. In fact, this book started out as me writing letters as a gift to my father and then took on a life of its own.

To come back to my story, the program for school drop-outs was picking up drop-outs sighted hanging around the mall and city hall and training them to work in a new bistro created by the city hall for the kids. Located in the city hall itself, it was run by the kids for the kids. The idea behind the project was that the kids could slowly work their way towards an apprentice program and learn skills to support themselves (and stay off the streets). I really liked the concept - it touched my heart since, having been in the same boat myself, I knew what those kids were going through and what sort of backgrounds they were from. I pledged the foundation's support to the project. It was called Kids in the Hall Bistro and was a resounding success. (Queen Elizabeth and Prince Phillip met the kids and staff and toured the program facilities when they visited Alberta for the Provinces Centennial Year two years later in 2005. And no, in case you're wondering, I wasn't around during their visit. I didn't get to know about it until the kids sent me photographs.)

SIXTY-SIX

People Bridge brought a lot of joy in my life. Interacting with the beneficiaries of our projects also taught me that money counts for very little. I met fun-loving, joyful people in the most challenging situations, singing in Africa, dancing in India. These exchanges helped me realize that people from developed countries in the West are very spoilt and often not aware of just how lucky they are. For instance, we don't have to carry drinking water for our family seven miles every day, day after day. Isn't that something to be grateful for?

I enjoyed every moment of my time I spent working for the foundation and didn't mind traveling to review our projects. Sure, I used to strike a balance between my business and the foundation work, and work, and my personal life. But then there came a time in my life when I sought every opportunity to travel for the foundation to get away from Toronto... and Gerry.

Yes, you read that right. I can't really pin-point when trouble began between Gerry and me, but as time went by, Gerry slowly lost interest in my life. He became depressed and moody and would sleep a lot. He also became increasingly critical of Julie. I recollect that in 2005, we moved into a large apartment on Elm Avenue. The apartment was gorgeous to look at, but functionally, nothing seemed to work. In some ways, this state of affairs was symbolic of the turn our relationship had taken. Things were no longer right.

I believe the root cause for the stubborn disconnect that crept up between us was the disparity in the turn of events in our respective professional careers - the fact that my business continued to do well while his business floundered.

Gerry had a manufacturing business which around the time we had met in 1986, employed 500 people. Then the era of outsourcing began as manufacturers and service providers grew wise to the need to take their work overseas to cheaper production centers in China and India. Business has always been a game of numbers, but as the world has increasingly grown flat, it has also become a struggle to find the cheapest source for products and services.

Gerry didn't seem to understand this and lost out by not outsourcing. As a result, I witnessed his business slowly slide downhill over three years until 2006, when he went through receivership. We moved into Walmer Road to save money and also to get out of the aesthetic but dysfunctional apartment on Elm Avenue. Our life had suddenly become very tough. Gerry owed huge sums of money, over and above, which he was paying his ex-wife a large alimony.

I had never been able to understand his financial set-up and this frustrated him - on my part, I had seen how messy his divorce had been and was really nervous about his ex-wife. I had realized back then that Gerry's way of dealing with money was very different from mine, and so I'd insisted that we keep our money separate. Thus, in a sense, it wasn't surprising that I couldn't offer him any help by way of solutions. To be fair to myself, since I realized that I couldn't help him sort out his finances, I suggested counseling or professional advice, but he was just not interested, flatly replying, "Nothing can be done."

That only helped the rift between us to grow.

SIXTY-SEVEN

I couldn't comprehend Gerry's attitude - it was so unlike my fix-every-wrong-that-appears-in-your-path approach to life.

In June 2007, I recollect we had traveled for a holiday to Sante Fe in New Mexico when our apartment was flooded due to leaky plumbing from two floors above us, which wasn't discovered for a week. What a mess! We had to move out while the place was cleaned up. Gerry chose to move to a hotel while I went ('ran away' is more like it) to Newfoundland. After spending a few months there, I decided to move to the country. I was sick of our situation and identified the city with a relationship gone sour. The countryside was not exactly an escape route, but a last-ditch effort to set things right between us.

I found a pretty little apartment in the country while Gerry chose to move into my old apartment on Balmoral Avenue. We saw less and less of each other but even then, our relationship didn't improve, it simply got worse. Those were trying times - I was always preoccupied trying to figure out what had gone wrong. Gerry would say that he would always love me, but that he couldn't handle me anymore (whatever that meant).

I responded in true style, as I've always done when up against sad episodes. I've found it hard to accept the end of relationships, and as a result, I've sought to hold on by trying to work things out even when it was evident that the relationship had nothing left in it.

Incidentally, there's nothing wise in the way I reacted. Over the years, I've learned a few things from my friends in the East, such as, in Far Eastern philosophy, the Tao symbolizes the natural way of life. I'd describe the Tao as the path of least resistance, of unconditionally accepting events taking place in your life and the world around you. In that sense, the Tao symbolizes a 'go with the flow' sort of lifestyle wherein you do not resist change. And since change is inevitable (Heraclitus, the Greek philosopher, said that change is the only constant in our lives), the Tao is hailed by Eastern mystics as the way to always be happy come what may. Of course, it's another matter that it isn't easy to live by the Tao - it can take some of us (the likes of me) a lifetime to learn to let go.

When I looked, I found more wisdom corroborating the Tao in medieval Catholic history. An oft-quoted prayer by Saint Francis of Assisi, the founder of the Franciscan order, goes, 'Lord grant me the serenity to accept the things I cannot change, the courage to change the things I can, and the wisdom to know the difference (between the two).'

Saint Francis's words of wisdom, which are as relevant today as when he first spoke the prayer around the year 1200 AD, suggest that it helps to make the most of what you have and not dwell on the many things you cannot change (or can't have). Spending your time and energy on thinking about 'what could have been... ' is a sheer waste. Besides, it makes you sad.

SIXTY-EIGHT

That leads me to think about the choices we make as we go about the journey called life. People around me have often turned around and told me that I'm lucky for having a perfect life. That's far-fetched, to say the least. If you think about it, is anyone blessed with a perfect life in our day and age? That would mean having it all - idyllic relationships, wealth to indulge your passions, good health, and no troubles whatsoever.

We all know the answer to that.

But maybe it's my approach to life that my friends appreciate. Sure, there's no such thing as a perfect life. And yet, if you were to ask me if my life is perfect, I'd resolutely answer in the affirmative because I think perceiving anything as being perfect is a state of mind. So - life is perfect if you make it out to be so.

If you can make the Tao and St Francis's path of acceptance as your own, you'll have taken the first step to see life as being perfect because that's the way to move on from the imperfections that blot your way. I know I've taken time to accept, but once I have, I've done so resolutely without ever looking back, determined to get past my darkest hours. I've stayed optimistic about the happiness that lies in store for me, around the next corner, and switched on the best in me to make my lows work for me. I've made three choices - acceptance, staying positive, and doing what it takes to make things work out - that have made my life perfect for me. That's about all you can do to stay happy when the going gets rough.

And yes, I also haven't whined about my fate to my friends. I think that's something they like about me too. The reason I don't complain is that I believe that we've all been dealt a hand and that every hand is a potential winner or loser... depending on how we play the game of life. I'm borrowing words from legendary country music crooner Kenny Rogers here. In *The Gambler*, Kenny sang about life, likening it to poker and defined some rules to play the game of life, 'You got to know when to hold 'em, know when to fold 'em, know when to walk away and know when to run. You never count your money when you're sittin' at the table. There'll be time enough for countin' when the dealin's done. Ev'ry gambler knows that the secret to survivin' is knowin' what to throw away and knowin' what to keep 'cause ev'ry hand's a winner and ev'ry hand's a loser...'

It's so true. Every hand is a potential winner or an impending loser. It all depends on how you play it when you're put to the test. That's why it's said that life is what you make of it, from the hand you first pick up until the last card is dealt. I also love Kenny's metaphor for knowing when to let go... know when to walk away, know when to run. It took me so long to know that I should walk away from Gerry. When things turned sour, I tried and tried to sort things out between us, and by doing so, only made things harder for myself.

Gerry had let his business define his persona, and when that fell apart, he felt that he had nothing left. But he was still driven to keep up a good front - buying prime seats to events, renewing his golf club membership and so on. Well, he succeeded alright, many people didn't know he had lost his business, and of course, they didn't know that he had fallen into a rut of despair, taking our relationship with him. His depression slowly led to temper tantrums - fist-pounding, yelling, fights, and all sorts of unpleasant reactions.

As a result, when we went out for dinner, I was always hoping that an opportunity to talk things over in a neutral setting would soothe his distraught mind; his anger always got in the way, leaving me with no choice but to back off. I was hurt and couldn't understand how love could end this way. It didn't seem fair.

Why was Gerry no longer present in the relationship?

Why didn't he want to sort himself out?

Why didn't 'us' matter to him any more?

It took me all of a year to accept that I couldn't hold on any longer. Finally, I let go of a relationship that had slipped out of my hands much earlier.

The months after we split were hard going. Gerry and I had to talk to each other fairly often since we had a lot of stuff to sort out - these interactions were most unpleasant. I could sense his anger within, and of course, his rage had to spill out on me. Gerry would lose no time in telling our friends that he had done everything I wanted, which was true, only he conveniently chose to overlook his own behavior. In spite of this, I was determined not to give him a reason to gripe about the way we parted. So I reckoned that I would do everything right as far as our split was concerned, such as clear out my things from his place in Florida and return a car he had gifted me. Sure, that made me look very stupid, but then, at least it brought me some peace of mind.

SIXTY-NINE

Although the decision to part with Gerry was my own, I felt miserable after we split. I was living in the country at the time. If at all, that made the going even more difficult - away from my friends, I moped alone.

It's not even as though I had my work to keep my mind occupied during this time. I'd hung up my boots a year earlier. Winding up Betty Steinhauer & Associates was a slow process as it transpired; over that time, each of my long-term clients with whom I had retainer agreements also shut shop. When I turned sixty, I'd decided that I wouldn't replace my retiring clients with new ones, but at the same time, I'd let the process of winding up my business affairs run its course. The foundation was also taking up a lot of my time around about then.

My business lasted all of twenty-four glorious years from 1983 to 2007. I'm grateful for the way things turned out. But I didn't want it to go on and on - I'm certainly not one of those people who want to keep on working until the day they die! I guess I don't fear retirement the way some people do. Coming to think of it, I don't even count the word 'retirement' as part of my lexicon.

As of now, I'm open to taking up short-term assignments if something interesting comes my way. Otherwise, I believe there are so many other things for me to do, like spend time with my grandchildren, travel, and find my own version of a mountain top to grow old on. That's why I no longer hanker for a busy professional life. I've been there, done that, and enjoyed it while it lasted.

To my mind, we have to enjoy every phase of life. To put that philosophically, I'd say that time is like a river... you can't touch the same water twice because it flows on and on. That's why I believe it is important to cherish every moment.

I whole-heartedly agree with Dr. Wayne Dyer, the best-selling author who is affectionately called the 'father of motivation' by his fans, who said, 'Stop acting as if life is a rehearsal. Live this day as though it were your last. The past is over and gone. The future is not guaranteed.'

Careers should be enjoyable - I know how much I value mine. But if you think of it, most of our adult lives are spent working. So I think we should look beyond work when we can afford to. Life isn't only about working and earning more, especially when good fortune has already shone its face upon you. I guess that's why I never thought of winding up my business as missing out on being in the limelight. What's there to miss? I've kept in touch with clients who grew to become my friends. And if you think of it, aren't people and relationships the mainstay of human existence? So considering all of that, I simply thought of winding up my business as entering a different phase of life, a time that would offer me a different kind of freedom, such as the freedom to travel without worrying about my clients, or the freedom to revisit my roots, or celebrate the oneness of humanity.

SEVENTY

As life goes on, I feel more and more a citizen of the world. Not Canadian and not British. I say British because I was born in Luton, Bedfordshire, England in... you don't really want to know, do you?... 1943. Yes. I'm a World War II baby, born during hard times.

Oh, I'm not trying to suggest that I felt the impact of the war, at the age of two. But somewhere in the farthermost recesses of my mind, I still vaguely recollect being carried down to the nearest air-raid shelter when the sirens went off, where I'd entertain myself by eating a lot of cookies as my mother sought to entertain me (and others) by singing *The bear went over the mountain* (it's funny, but as I sit and write this, I realize I turned out to be a lot like that bear, wandering over many mountain tops to indulge my passion for travel, never tiring of taking in the sights and sounds of our world).

My father, Percy Axtell, a mechanic, was serving in the Home Guard when I was born. My mother, Christine Richardson, was a stay-at-home mum. She, poor woman, suffered badly from rheumatoid arthritis and took sick very often. Jim and Lucy, a nice couple who lived next door, would step in and babysit whenever Mum was down. And that was pretty often.

I think that's why when Britons began to pick up the threads of their lives after the war ended, it struck my father that something was still not going for us - England's damp climate never had and never would suit my mother. I now understand that he must have thought that relocating to a new land would offer my ailing mother a fresh start. Away from the dampness, she might feel healthier and be able to look after me better. Dad began looking for opportunities in Canada and soon bagged a job as a machine foreman with a leading tire manufacturing company in Toronto. That clinched it.

My small family - my parents and I - migrated to Canada. We crossed the Atlantic in the Queen Elizabeth II, setting sail for new horizons. I was four.

I revisited England two decades later when I was in my twenties. I met up with Jim and Lucy, and they were thrilled to see me, to see how I'd turned out. It was a timely visit because they both died the year after. I was so glad I made the trip, inspired by a gut feeling to travel back to my roots. Not that I had any family other than Jim and Lucy to look up. My father was the youngest of thirteen siblings born to parents who were both blind, but we had not kept in touch with any of his extended family, and much earlier, while my father was still alive, I'd heard that most of my uncles had passed away.

SEVENTY-ONE

I feel that I'm a citizen of this world because my heart says that we (humanity) are one family - a lot more unites us than the differences of opinion that divide us. I know it doesn't always seem that way, especially when people fight in the name of religion. But it is so.

Each of People Bridge's projects reinforced my belief in the oneness of the human race. Truly, there should be no boundaries, no separations, and no dissent because people are essentially the same all over the world. And yet, we're surrounded by nothing short of madness... terrorism threatens our survival as never before.

To make some sense of it all and to spend time in England (which I love), I decided to take a one-week course in comparative religion in Oxford in the spring of 2008. I was the only woman and non-member of some clergy or the other doing the course, so I got to hear a lot of interesting views.

I chose the course thinking that it would help me understand other religions and be more respectful of peoples' beliefs. And I thought it might help me come to terms with the concept of heaven and hell, something that was ingrained in me as a child but that I still struggle to accept - I have a problem understanding how decisions are made about heaven and hell in terms of who goes where.

Staying in Oxford was fun too. I rented a little flat on the river and spent my days walking, riding a bike, visiting the art movie house, shopping in the local market, taking the bus or train to London to catch up with friends, and at the Oxford Center of the Brahma Kumaris. Plus, my friend Cathi from Labrador, Canada, stayed with me for a few days. I really enjoyed being part of the community.

SEVENTY-TWO

Oxford was a much-needed getaway for me. But when I got back to Toronto, my spirits were still low. Perhaps that's why I let my friend Elaine talk me into taking a cruise together. She said I needed a change. She was right. I also saw her suggestion as an opportunity to open my eyes to more newness.

We set sail for a 110-day round-the-world cruise on January 19, 2009. Here are some of the cruise notes I kept and sent to friends:

January 19

I met Hal, an eighty-year-old gentleman from Miami, Florida. He seems to be a very interesting person. I first saw him at the reception desk asking for help with his emails because he has macular degeneration in his eyes. The girl at the reception wasn't too helpful, so I offered to help out. If nothing else, I'm sure he'll have some interesting stories to share!

January 29

We are in Lima, Peru, for the day, en route to Easter Island. So far, I am really enjoying this trip. I have a trainer and am actually learning kickboxing! My BlackBerry should work for the next couple of days, as long as we are coasting South America. After that, it'll be back to using the ships' computers, speaking of which I have been meeting Hal every day for his emails. I think he is very bright and has done some very interesting things in his personal and professional life.

February 3

Here I am at Easter Island. In all of my travels, I have never seen such blue water as we have been treated to in the last couple of days (deep royal or marine blue). Easter Island is home to about 3,000 people, most of whom have never left the island, possibly because it is said to be the most remote inhabited island in the world. Anyway, they seem so well settled in what I can only describe as an idyllic existence. Perhaps that is why they never think of stepping out of their cocoon?

I have just finished a course on art history on board - the lectures were superb. And guess what, the Super Bowl was transmitted by special satellite to the ship. I couldn't miss watching it - the excitement was palpable and very infectious even though I had no clue which teams were playing!

February 16

We have had no access to CNN for the last 10 days, just FOX, so we have set up a lobby to get it back! I had an opportunity to chat with several guests who have also sailed on freighters. Hmmm, maybe that is something I will consider for my next trip?

Oh, and by the way, I really admire my new friend Hal. I got to know about his eye problem because I overheard his conversation with the receptionist. But if it were not for that, I wouldn't have a clue about it because he handles his ocular disability and his pacemaker really well. Like he never misses a pretty woman walking by, which just goes to show... !

March 1

We will be leaving Australia tomorrow. I visited Sydney, Brisbane, and Cairns (the Great Barrier Reef). I was amazed at what I saw when I was here a number of years ago. I am as amazed this time. Today, I actually went snorkeling, which wasn't easy because I don't swim, so they tied me to a length of rope and let me go – it sounds as funny as it felt! But it worked!

Our next stop is Papua New Guinea. I hope I have a better time than my last visit when I had to bribe my way out of the country!

March 7

We stopped at Rabaul, Papua New Guinea, where we learned that the township is built on an active volcano - it last erupted in 1994. I found it very sad to see people living on top of solidified layers of lava, knowing fully well that scores of homes and people lay buried beneath. The area grows no crops; there is no vegetation to speak of, and so, no fields for livestock to graze in. People travel miles to buy supplies. And yet they have chosen to live on a volcano. I can tell you that set me thinking, as a result of which I was very upset when I got back on the ship, where Hal treated me to two Margaritas to cheer me up! Well, that was the end of me for a while. When I recovered, I sat and wrote some postcards to my grandchildren. I know I sound very depressed about what I saw. Well, I was. My train of thought led me to decide that I would seriously take up the pen and write my memoirs. God knows how I was inspired to help the less privileged. Perhaps I can inspire others to do so too? In any case, as many of you know, I have been meaning to write my memoirs for many years. Well, I am on the job now and writing every day. And thanks to Hal, I have the perfect place to write, watching the sea. He leaves the ship off and on for various excursions and has offered me his balcony room to use whenever he is not on board. It is very peaceful in his room, much quieter than mine since I have a roommate.

March 16

I enjoyed our two stops in Japan - Hiroshima, and Osaka. I also visited Kyoto, which I would love to revisit. Now, we are on our way to Seoul, Korea.

Cruising is a great way to see the world! Not that I am a novice at that, having visited 150-odd countries. But I have learned so much on this trip alone - sailing through the Tasman Sea, the Coral Sea, the Yellow Sea, and China Sea, plus the Mariana Trench (the deepest known point of the world's oceans) - about wind, waves, docking, ports and the Equator, which we have crossed twice. The educational program on board continues to be superb! We now have a former CIA agent with us. He was posted in Russia. His tales leave us spellbound!

Guess what? My trip is half over, and I'm still here!!

March 22

China was wow! The country has changed so much since my first visit. As I took in the sights and sounds of Shanghai, I found it very easy to understand why the West is losing it - China is building new infrastructure at a crazy pace. There are cranes all over the place! True to my nature, I decided to help the Chinese economy some more by shopping big time! And our sailing out of Hong Kong was an extremely memorable experience - the passengers were treated to a light show on the tallest of buildings. It was spectacular!

March 24

I watched the sunrise from the upper deck. We were surrounded by fishing boats making their way from the mouth of the Mekong River into the China Sea. I found myself pinching myself. Truly this is a hard-to-believe trip!

I should also mention that I've grown fairly close to Hal over the past few weeks. I've discovered that he looked after his sickly wife for the last fifteen years of her life after she had a stroke and was incapacitated - isn't that honorable? That meant retiring early from his professional life; he was a successful land and real estate developer in Miami.

Hal has a very quick mind, is curious and fun to be with, and is witty. Plus, he is a very dapper dresser. Everything must match, and it all has to be crowned with a matching cap. He says that he has at least 50 caps from all over the world, not baseball caps, proper caps. No, I haven't asked him how many he's brought with him to the ship! Our daily meetings to sort out his emails have evolved to sharing a glass of champagne every evening before dinner (as we have different dinner sittings) or brandy after dinner. Hmmm, I find myself acknowledging that Hal is very charming and gracious. But I'm not looking to get involved, am I? And as far as I can reckon, neither is he... Well, we'll see what the future brings.

March 26

Ho Chi Minh City was very hot and has changed immensely since my first visit years ago. It has become very busy now, and several Western-style hotels have come up. I went shopping for clothes but found nothing of my size. Everything on the racks was a size 2 - that's far too small!

Cambodia is the land of gentle people, and I also had the opportunity to catch up with representatives of an ongoing People Bridge project, which I was informed is progressing well. And I indulged myself too, by having a massage on the beach. Wow! Seventy-five minutes for only 35 dollars.

March 30

We visited Singapore - I call the city one big shopping mall. Hal and I went to Raffles, the famous hotel, intending to have Singapore Slings (they were invented here, but I still don't think that justifies the cost - $27 apiece!) with a great lunch! We also spent a day in Kuala Lumpur. Now we are on our way to Port Blair, the capital city of the Andaman Islands, 600 miles off the coast of India, before we make our way to Mumbai, where I hear the temperature is 40 degrees. Phew!

April 7

Here I am in Mumbai, having sailed around the southern tip of India from the Andaman Islands. I have a bad cold, so I planned to spend a quiet day in Mumbai. I hired a car and driver to take me to the Taj Hotel, as I was keen to see the place after the terror attacks - I was shocked to see the extent of the damage. Still, I had a great manicure and pedicure for only $26 - the ship charges a fortune for the same! Treatments at the Taj are truly the best, what with the roses and perfume and all that jazz!

We are off to Dubai now!

April 11

You may find this interesting. We are sailing along the east coast of Oman in the Arabian Sea, an area infested with pirates. The Captain was briefed by the Royal Navy yesterday in Dubai. Apparently, we are very low-risk because these pirates target expensive cargo, not passenger liners. But the Captain is taking no chances as a result of which we will be put through an anti-piracy drill tomorrow. Plus, we have protection from the navies of India, the UK, and the USA. They've surrounded us with what they call war canoes, which just look like large ships to my eyes! Not to mention that the Canadian and USA armies are doing flyovers - it's all happening for real! I feel as though I'm an actor shooting for a war movie!!

Do you know - Mr. Larger-Than-Life Hal is eighty years old, which makes him fourteen years older than me. I must confess that we are officially seeing each other, speaking of which we have this joke between us - he is the oldest man I have gone out with, and I am the oldest woman he has gone out with! You wouldn't believe his age unless he told you, he is in very good shape; and actually does Tai Chi for one hour every morning without fail.

April 19

It took us two days to get through the Gulf of Aden. We were part of a convoy that included British, Indian, and USA warships, and we sailed at our highest speed to reach certain checkpoints. Looking forward to Egypt, where a group of us (including Hal) are taking a three-day overland trip to Karnak and Abu Simbel to see the pyramids. Apparently, we will have to travel with armed security. Alas, it seems to have become the way of the world!

April 22

Wow! We visited Luxor, the Valley of the Kings, the Aswan Dam, Abu Simbel, and Cairo, where we saw the pyramids and a mind-blowing mummy exhibit!! During the tour, Hal, the old romantic, in a very timely manner (I must say) both for the reference to Egypt and to the much-traveled beloved (me!), decided that Jo Stafford's You Belong To Me is our song, so when it played this evening, I appreciated it even more than I normally do:

See the pyramids along the Nile
Watch the sun rise on a tropic isle
But just remember, darling, all the while
You belong to me...

We're on our way to Europe now. There are only sixteen (precious) days left of this most amazing journey. The best part is that I have so much to look forward to after the cruise is over. Hal and I will be spending time doing things together. Oh, I do realize that nothing is for sure in this world (after all, Hal is 80). And I would be very sad if he died before me, but what matters is that we are enjoying our time together now. And Hal is very supportive; I think he has come into my life at the right time, plus he is a refreshing change from Gerry. I'm working on the first draft of my autobiography and Hal is so interested in everything that is being written. I read him my work every night, and he makes suggestions, which is great.

April 29

We sailed past Istanbul in the last few days. Our last few ports will be Venice, Messina, Sicily, Barcelona, and Cannes, because this amazing journey will be over on May 8 when we dock in Rome.

I will leave this ship with mixed emotions. We have become a small global community. Of the 600 original passengers on board, 400 of us took the world cruise. For me, the bonus of the trip is undoubtedly meeting Hal - he is very supportive and unlike any other man I have seen.

It was also great to get news from back home and from friends around the world these past months when I was sailing – thank you all so much for keeping in touch by email and phone. I hope to see many of you very soon plus get back to some type of normalcy for me. Whatever that is!!!

***

I traveled a lot in 2009. After the cruise, I went off to Iceland - the country was picturesque - and then I made my way to Greenland, where I realized that Iceland is not a patch on the latter. Greenland is a land of such phenomenal beauty and boasts of excellent tourist infrastructure to showcase its best points. You can fly over glaciers at a low altitude in small (eight-seater) passenger planes, for instance.

Then Hal was inspired to travel some more too, instead of staying around in Florida where I used to visit him every now and then. I made friends with his children, and they were all very gracious towards me. Tracy, in her 40s, has a disease that affects her speech and movement. She is one of the greatest spirits I have ever met, and I'm glad to be her friend.

So Hal and I traveled together on four more cruises! Over the course of a year, we traveled to the Caribbean, northern New England in the United States, South America, and Antarctica. It was the last continent left for me to visit. Call it the final frontier - and it lived up to every expectation I had about it in spite of the intense cold, the unpredictable weather, and the icebergs floating past the ship. I have seen much beauty in the world, but never anything like Antarctica. What with the whales in the distance, and the seals and penguins beckoning on the shores, and the albatrosses soaring majestically above us, I felt as though I were on a different planet.

Hal was very funny on this cruise; remember he was from Florida, so not used to cold weather. On this cruise, he just wouldn't venture outside our cabin in spite of having the best waterproof clothes that money can buy. The only time he relented was to have his picture taken against the enchanting backdrop... all you can see of him in the photograph is his nose!

Sailing to Antarctica was special because it set my mind at ease during a time when I was thinking deeply about the next stage in my life. My working career was over, Gerry and I had broken up, and I was settled in a new (rented) apartment in downtown Toronto. I'd also wound up the ongoing projects of People Bridge. Not because it wasn't doing well, no. Quite the contrary. I'm proud of what we have achieved in a short span of time - we funded over one hundred projects in just over a decade and last year, counted sixty, of our donors as strangers who saw the benefit in our work.

In fact, I'd like to take this opportunity to thank everyone who pitched in along the way and helped us reach this far - together, we performed the impossible. The foundation introduced me to our project partners and beneficiaries in a number of countries across the globe. I feel blessed to know these large-hearted people. Many of my trips have been difficult - the traveling has been dusty and uncomfortable, and I've not always had a decent bathroom to use or food to my liking, but people have gone out of their way to share the best of what they have, and you really can't ask for more than that, can you?

Coming back to my story, I just felt that it was time to release myself of responsibilities that tied me down. So I freed myself, and then was uncertain about what to expect next and somewhat worried about my future, especially because of my intrinsic nature to set sail (metaphorically speaking) in uncharted waters.

Then, one evening, as Hal and I enjoyed dinner in the warmth of our cabin looking out on beautiful and majestic Antarctica, he affectionately told me that he expected to look down from heaven years from now to see me, a very old woman, trying to figure out her next adventure.

I laughed to hear him say that. Then I realized how well he'd come to know me during the months we spent together. And surprisingly, the feeling that had been lurking in me subsided. Hal's words brought me round to accepting that I can't really change my basic nature. I'm spontaneous. I'm adventurous. I'm free-spirited. So be it.

It came to my mind that you can't change your basic nature, and you can't change the hand you were dealt with when you were born and many of the situations you find yourself in. But the way to react to life is in your hands - you can decide when to walk or run away from situations, or when to hold on and give it your best shot. Better still, you can choose how you want to see the world - whether you want to continue seeing it the way you were brought up to or get a fresh pair of eyes to see it anew.

It also came to my mind that I was worrying because I was scared that as I got older, I may no longer have been able to keep up with the lifestyle I'd gotten used to... when a new idea just has to take me by surprise, popping into my head as though out of the blue, and... voila! I embark on an adventure or raise funds to help people. It's not like I'm afraid of death - as far as I am concerned, if I were to die tomorrow, I would be mad about what I was going to miss in life. But I would rest peacefully, happy and content about the way that I lived my life, and if you think of it, isn't that what counts?

SEVENTY-THREE

The more I think about death, I believe the spirit within lives on (and hopefully, if you've led a decent life, more than you, the values that drove you will be remembered and celebrated). The uncertainty of life also drives me to not want to put off for tomorrow what I can do today, such as thank everyone who has ever been a part of my life and enriched it in some way.

But of course, I wouldn't want to be dependent on my children in my old age. Jody has her hands full as it is, what with her family and business. And Julie, well, she's undoubtedly a special person even if she goes about life in an unconventional manner... but I hope she realizes that she is sometimes her own enemy... such as when she separated with George after being married for ten years. It's a pity she didn't value him because he was a really good influence on her and encouraged her to take up the position of a waitress in a restaurant and slowly climb the ranks to a managerial position.

All said and done, I'm proud of both my girls. They're independent women, yes, Julie too, even if she hops from job to job making just about enough money. I'd like to think that I had something to do with the way they turned out, probably because being a normal housewife was never my thing, and maybe, somewhere deep down, I still feel guilty about chasing my own needs. In fact, if you were to ask me what legacy I leave my children and grandchildren, it's just 'Enjoy life. Never say never - stay open to new things. Be curious!'

SEVENTY-FOUR

I write this sitting in a little room in Doctor's House, the guest house of the Global Hospital in Mount Abu. It's about a mile away from the room I first stayed in, as a guest of the Brahma Kumaris. My relationship with the Brahma Kumaris continues, and I genuinely hope that they will always be a part of my life, in some way or the other. I have no idea if they will mean more or less in the future - my guess, however, is more!

I keep coming back to India, and within it, to Mount Abu, to my wonderful friends within this socio-spiritual organization. They're inspiring people who've worked on themselves and figured out a lot of things that must make sense to them. In future, their lifestyle may appeal to me too. Ant says to me that now that I'm growing old (hardly but whatever), celibacy will begin to make sense to me... He makes me sound as though I'm addicted to sex, which is so not true... especially now that I'm beginning to think more deeply about the point of being in a relationship.

Writing this book has been useful in that respect. It's probably the closest I could ever come to doing a life review, and it's showed me just how much I need to work on myself, if for nothing else, then for the sake of being in a perfect relationship, something I've always aspired to experience. Now, more than ever before, I realize that the perfect relationship is the outcome of two wholes coming together, not two halves trying to make it work. There'll always be something missing when two halves get together, even if they don't realize it themselves.

Take my relationship with Jahangir, my soulmate. I used to think that was as close as I'd ever gotten to a perfect relationship, but I'm not so sure about that now. While I was writing this book, I found out that Jahangir was survived by a wife and that she still lives in Mumbai. A wife. Ouch.

When I first learned about his marital status, I exclaimed: 'Oh my God, he was so good at hiding the truth.'

Other than that, I was cool about it, probably because a lot of water has passed under the bridge in the last decade, and I guess I have been working on myself a little.

I know many people around me see me as being strong and in control and needing no support. But I know better. Beneath the surface, there's this woman who's always wanted to be cared for and loved. For many years, I had a cute magnet stuck to my fridge - it said, 'In my next life I want to come back as a Barbie Doll.' I think that sums up how I felt - vulnerable and seeking love from without.

But now, I want to feel full, full within myself, not because of the way a man can make me feel. I want to be as complete, as perfect, as any human being can be. That way, if I ever do enter into another relationship, it'll hopefully be because I'm attracted to someone who is also very much his own person, not someone who shows an interest in fulfilling my needs - that's always a temporary thing. Then, we can champion one another.

It's pouring outside - unexpected weather for November when the sun should be shining and the skies a brilliant clear blue, not murky grey. Global warming is making itself felt more and more, and how. I smile to see two cows huddling under the shelter of a big tree outside my window. Cows-on-the-road is so typical of India, a place that is the real deal for me. I'm amazed at how the country has changed since my first trip two decades ago. Many people in the West identify India with the country's prowess in information technology, but if you think of the call center industry in context with the country as a whole, it is a very small facet of modern India. As far as I'm concerned, in spite of my having traversed almost the entire length and breadth of the country and seen its diverse cultures and traditions, it remains a perennial mystery. India always has a card up its sleeve, so to speak, and reveals some magic, newness, and a lot of wisdom every time I visit it. It inspires me - that's why this account of my life started en route to India. And that's also why I choose to sign off here.

EPILOGUE

I spent a lot of time with Hal up until mid-2010. We would stay in touch even when I wasn't in Florida, talking twice a day when I was in Canada and once a day when I was traveling. I must admit though, sometimes I felt the pressure to call him when he wanted me to, at his time. One day he called me, furious about the fact that he didn't know where I was and what I was doing. That saddened me. I couldn't be what he wanted, nor could I spend more time with him in Florida. So we stopped seeing one another.

In the ensuing year, one of his children called me to tell me that he was very unwell. Hal died a few weeks after that, the fourth man in my life to have passed away.

Hal was my last relationship. I have male friends in my life but I don't feel the need for a relationship. There was a time in my life when I couldn't have imagined reaching this stage but there you are. I am now very much my own person. Spirituality interests me. So does travel, and my love for adventure is intact.

Occasionally my thoughts gravitate towards the inevitability of death and almost always immediately thereafter, to the need to celebrate life. Remember the Frank Sinatra number, It was a very good year. I'd like to think that way for my own life at the end, that they were years well spent. And I will.

POSTSCRIPT

To my Dad

You gave me strength of character and taught me how to be a survivor. Mom just didn't know how to move on and press forward with life. I learned that from you, and if you hadn't given me that, I could have ended up like Mom - STUCK FOREVER.

If you are looking at me from above, thank you for everything you gave me in our very short time together, and please know that I feel very sorry for Mom. You were her strength and anchor. I didn't understand that for many years, to be honest, not until this book happened.

Your daughter,

Betty

www.ingramcontent.com/pod-product-compliance
Lightning Source LLC
LaVergne TN
LVHW041155080426
835511LV00006B/603